Montserrat

WORLD BIBLIOGRAPHICAL SERIES

General Editors:
Robert G. Neville (Executive Editor)
John J. Horton

Robert A. Myers   Ian Wallace
Hans H. Wellisch   Ralph Lee Woodward, Jr.

John J. Horton is Deputy Librarian of the University of Bradford and currently Chairman of its Academic Board of Studies in Social Sciences. He has maintained a longstanding interest in the discipline of area studies and its associated bibliographical problems, with special reference to European Studies. In particular he has published in the field of Icelandic and of Yugoslav studies, including the two relevant volumes in the World Bibliographical Series.

Robert A. Myers is Associate Professor of Anthropology in the Division of Social Sciences and Director of Study Abroad Programs at Alfred University, Alfred, New York. He has studied post-colonial island nations of the Caribbean and has spent two years in Nigeria on a Fulbright Lectureship. His interests include international public health, historical anthropology and developing societies. In addition to *Amerindians of the Lesser Antilles: a bibliography* (1981), *A Resource Guide to Dominica, 1493–1986* (1987) and numerous articles, he has compiled the World Bibliographical Series volumes on *Dominica* (1987) and *Nigeria* (1989).

Ian Wallace is Professor of German at the University of Bath. A graduate of Oxford in French and German, he also studied in Tübingen, Heidelberg and Lausanne before taking teaching posts at universities in the USA, Scotland and England. He specializes in contemporary German affairs, especially literature and culture, on which he has published numerous articles and books. In 1979 he founded the journal *GDR Monitor*, which he continues to edit under its new title *German Monitor*.

Hans H. Wellisch is Professor emeritus at the College of Library and Information Services, University of Maryland. He was President of the American Society of Indexers and was a member of the International Federation for Documentation. He is the author of numerous articles and several books on indexing and abstracting, and has published *The Conversion of Scripts* and *Indexing and Abstracting: an International Bibliography*. He also contributes frequently to *Journal of the American Society for Information Science, The Indexer* and other professional journals.

Ralph Lee Woodward, Jr. is Chairman of the Department of History at Tulane University, New Orleans, where he has been Professor of History since 1970. He is the author of *Central America, a Nation Divided*, 2nd ed. (1985), as well as several monographs and more than sixty scholarly articles on modern Latin America. He has also compiled volumes in the World Bibliographical Series on *Belize* (1980), *Nicaragua* (1983), and *El Salvador* (1988). Dr. Woodward edited the Central American section of the *Research Guide to Central America and the Caribbean* (1985) and is currently editor of the Central American history section of the *Handbook of Latin American Studies*.

VOLUME 134

Montserrat

Riva Berleant-Schiller

Compiler

CLIO PRESS

OXFORD, ENGLAND · SANTA BARBARA, CALIFORNIA
DENVER, COLORADO

British Library Cataloguing in Publication Data

Berleant-Schiller, Riva
Montserrat. – (World bibliographical series; 134)
I. Title
016.72975

ISBN 1–85109–154–8

Clio Press Ltd.,
55 St. Thomas' Street,
Oxford OX1 1JG, England.

ABC-CLIO,
130 Cremona Drive,
Santa Barbara,
CA 93117, USA.

Designed by Bernard Crossland.
Typeset by Columns Design and Production Services, Reading, England.
Printed and bound in Great Britain by
Billing and Sons Ltd., Worcester.

THE WORLD BIBLIOGRAPHICAL SERIES

This series, which is principally designed for the English speaker, will eventually cover every country (and many of the world's principal regions), each in a separate volume comprising annotated entries on works dealing with its history, geography, economy and politics; and with its people, their culture, customs, religion and social organization. Attention will also be paid to current living conditions – housing, education, newspapers, clothing, etc.– that are all too often ignored in standard bibliographies; and to those particular aspects relevant to individual countries. Each volume seeks to achieve, by use of careful selectivity and critical assessment of the literature, an expression of the country and an appreciation of its nature and national aspirations, to guide the reader towards an understanding of its importance. The keynote of the series is to provide, in a uniform format, an interpretation of each country that will express its culture, its place in the world, and the qualities and background that make it unique. The views expressed in individual volumes, however, are not necessarily those of the publisher.

VOLUMES IN THE SERIES

For Montserratians everywhere

Contents

Contents

Contents

Introduction

For anyone who troubles to look beyond the beach, the islands of the Caribbean, and especially the small ones of the Lesser Antillean chain, are at once compelling and bewildering. Though travel brochures promote a bland pastiche of sun and sand, the region offers much more to the curious and perceptive. Certainly the beauties of the islands are attractive, but equally commanding, in a more painful way, are the economic processes and historical circumstances that helped to shape regional social structure and a distinctive regional culture – colonial conquest; the destruction of native peoples; plantation economies and their drastic ecological alterations; slavery; the meeting of African, European, and native American cultures; stratification, poverty, and inequality; and the flow of people in and out of the islands and the region. However, even while we wonder at the regional conditions from which Caribbean peoples fashioned a pan-Caribbean adaptation with many widespread features, we are bewildered by the range and variety of islands, each with its own distinctive flavour. Understanding the dialectic between island particularity and pan-Caribbean commonality is critical to understanding both the region and any single island.

Montserrat is distinctive and intriguing, even while it is unmistakably Caribbean. The details of its history, ecology, and present circumstances are legion. Yet the same may be said of any Lesser Antillean island, which surely enhances rather than diminishes the interest of both the region and its separate islands. It is important, therefore, in this brief introduction to the island, to balance regional and particular, and to consider first the general features of Caribbean history and environment into which Montserrat may be fitted. Then, against a background of Caribbean commonality, the special character and circumstances of the island can be illuminated.

Landscape and Physical Setting

As a group, the Lesser Antillean islands were formed by volcanic and seismic processes in an unstable region of the earth's crust. Most of the volcanic mountain-building in the region had been completed by the Miocene era, but some volcanic activity still goes on, and Montserrat is one of the islands where there are active fumaroles and where eruption is still a distinct possibility. The 1930s and 1960s both saw periods of increased tremors and fumarole activity, though there was no eruption or earthquake.

During Pleistocene and Holocene or recent times, volcanic activity has declined and processes of uplift, tilting, reef-building, and erosion have modified the Antillean islands. These modifications of Miocene orogenesis have produced the present variety of island forms. One way of ordering the physical and geographical variety of the Lesser Antilles is to think of higher and lower, wetter and drier islands. Rainfall increases with altitude in the Caribbean, so that the low islands shaped by coral reef-building (examples are Barbados, St. Maarten, and Barbuda) are drier than the mountainous islands of volcanic origin. Montserrat falls in the latter group, although the risk of drought is always present, especially in the northern part of the island where the hills are very low. Other examples of high, wetter islands of the Lesser Antilles, many of them wetter than Montserrat, are Dominica, Grenada, Martinique, Nevis, and St. Lucia. There is considerable rainfall variation from year to year in each island and these variations even extend to the generally wetter islands.

The major influence on the weather of the Lesser Antilles is the trade wind system. The trades bring generally fair weather and a tropical climate nearly all-year round, interrupted by seasonal rainfall and by the hurricane season of June to November. Within this pattern there are individual island variations and island mosaics that result from differences in local topography. In Montserrat, the three prominent volcanic structures that increase in height from north to south are associated with marked differences in rainfall and humidity, and therefore in vegetation. The low Silver Hills region of the north is comparatively dry and its vegetation is adapted to dry conditions. Within a few kilometers are higher peaks that support rain forest.

Most of the Caribbean landscape that we see today is a human creation. Deforestation, subsistence cultivation, plantation agriculture, erosion, and the introduction of many species of plants and domesticated grazing animals from Europe, Asia, and Africa have shaped the land and its plant communities. Helmut Blume's standard geography of the region adopts the common classification for tropical American elevation zones and describes the plant communities characteristic of each. The highest zone, *tierra fria* (above 2,000 metres) is absent from the Lesser Antilles. The lowest, *tierra caliente*, which rises to 900 metres, bears a great variety of plant communities that range from thorn scrub and succulents to deciduous and semi-evergreen forests. These reflect moisture variations. The middle zone, *tierra templada*, bears some elfin woodlands. In Montserrat, the highest peaks of the Centre Hills do not rise above 800 metres, so that strictly speaking all of Montserrat falls into Blume's lowest zone. Nevertheless, Montserrat's complex mosaic of terrain, rainfall, and human agency on the land have created many microclimatic niches that support a range of plant communities. The higher peaks bear deciduous and semi-evergreen forest, rain forest, and elfin woodland, whereas much of the north is dry scrub and cactus.

The land itself carries the marks of cultivation and grazing. There are a few small terraced areas but the most typical vistas are of hillsides altered by the cross-slope shaping of garden plots into parallel ridges and troughs, and the delta-like accumulations of alluvium at the bottoms of plots, where even the ridges could not stop the downward wash of soil. Even slopes that are now uncultivated show these marks of abandoned gardens. In the north, the grazing of cattle, sheep, and goats has probably intensified the effects of drought periods and encouraged the spread of dry scrub vegetation.

History and Society

Archaeological research into the inhabitants of the Lesser Antilles before the European invasion in 1492 has burgeoned in the last twenty years. Still, there are great differences in our knowledge about the prehistory of individual islands. In general, sparse groups of Archaic peoples appear to have occupied the Lesser Antilles earlier than 2,000 years ago. Archaic sites are marked by tools of ground stone and the beginning of pottery making. Slightly less than 2,000 years ago the Saladoid people, identified by the style and quality of their ceramics, entered the Lesser Antilles from northern South America and apparently spread rapidly.

Montserrat is one of the few islands of the Lesser Antilles that have undergone systematic archaeological survey. The continuing work of archaeologist David Watters steadily expands our knowledge of

Introduction

Montserratian prehistory. Montserrat has several Saladoid sites, the earliest of which appears to be about 1,800 years old. The Post-Saladoid people, identified by the thicker, heavier body of their pottery material and its roughened surface without polychrome decoration, are represented by sites dating after about 1,000 years ago. Most of these sites indicate that their occupants chose low elevations, easy access to streams, proximity to the coast, and lands made suitable for cultivation by adequate soils and rainfall.

When Europeans arrived after 1492, they found a horticultural people called the Caribs distributed throughout the Lesser Antilles. The Caribs had apparently replaced the Arawaks, who continued to occupy the Greater Antilles. The site of a large Carib food garden is identifiable in Montserrat today. The European invasion, bringing conquest, slavery, disease, and demoralization, reduced the Carib population to a tenth of its numbers by 1550. Nevertheless, Carib raiding remained a dangerous nuisance to European intruders in Montserrat almost to the end of the seventeenth century.

Although Montserrat had been sighted and named by Columbus before 1500, no permanent European settlement began until 1632. The seventeenth century records in Montserrat have all been gradually destroyed by damp, insects, and hurricanes, so that we hardly know what treasures have been lost. Notwithstanding this, manuscript sources in Great Britain, comparative study of seventeenth-century observers' accounts, historical archaeology, and historical geography have all contributed to the piecemeal process which has contributed to our understanding of the early colonial period. Much has been made – and much nonsense – of the undoubted fact that among the earliest European settlers were Irish Catholics from the neighbouring island of St. Christopher. Why they came is not yet known. Suggestions include overpopulation in St. Christopher, exile from that island founded on prejudice against them, banishment as punishment for insubordination, and voluntary removal for the sake of religious freedom.

In this first period of settlement Montserrat was, like the other 'Caribbees' that later became the English Leeward Islands Colony, primarily a site for the production of tobacco on small holdings. Its initial settlement and earliest population were different, however, and one of the questions posed by the study of Montserrat is whether the ethnic, religious, and political characteristics of the early Montserratian population as a whole had any effects beyond the first settlement period, or whether the plantation economy eventually overwhelmed them, just as it overwhelmed the physical and biotic differences between islands and their early small-scale economies. Every writer on Montserrat from the seventeenth century onwards makes a point of mentioning the Irish settlement, but the significance of this for Montserrat's later history has always been more assumed than assessed. Sugar plantations were the great levellers in the Caribbean, wiping out distinctions and creating in the islands the requisite social and physical conditions for the production of sugar. Any argument in favour of perpetual Irish influence on Montserrat is yet to be supported by convincing evidence that takes into account the features of pan-Caribbean culture that Montserrat demonstrably shares with many sister islands. The only shreds of Irish culture that survive from Montserrat's past are place names and surnames, and these are by no means unique in the former British Caribbean. Otherwise, Montserratian culture is thoroughly Afro-Caribbean, despite the contemporary appropriation of conventionally Irish symbols such as the shamrock and the epithet 'emerald isle' that are designed to attract tourists.

Whatever the initial circumstances, the years from 1632 to about 1670 may be considered to be the first phase of European settlement which saw the beginning of a set of human-land relationships that were very different from the Amerindian relationships that preceded them. The earliest Europeans were food and tobacco farmers. Sugar plantations were present by 1649 but another half century passed before they came to dominate both economy and society. By 1660 some social and ecological relationships were starting to take shape around sugar production but sugar planters did not yet form a powerful class and the incipient plantation economy was almost wiped out in the French Wars of 1666-67.

Economic reconstruction and a greater metropolitan interest in Montserrat both began around 1670, once the wars were over, and 1670 to 1684 was the period during which a controlling planter class began to emerge in a society that still retained a rough frontier quality. By 1705, this planter class and a society based fully on slave labour and monocrop sugar production was fully established.

We might well ask how a plantation society is to be judged as such. Obvious questions deal with land use, the labour force, exports, source of income to the colony, and political control. What, for example, is the percentage of cultivated land devoted to sugar? What is produced on the rest and to what use is the product put? What percentage of the labour force is involved, directly or indirectly, in sugar production? In what hands is individual wealth concentrated? What percentage of the colony's income is derived from the plantation crop? Where is the locus of political and decision-making power? Who has authority and who has power? Are offices concentrated in planter hands? The point at which the plantation crop dominates the economy, and the planters become not merely planters, but a dominant class that controls political organization as well as the basic production is the point at which we may say there is a plantation society. From 1684 to 1705 this kind of society unmistakably took shape in Montserrat.

The eighteenth century was the century of prosperity for Montserrat and for her sister islands in Britain's Leeward Island Colony. The recruitment of indentured European labour had already declined seriously by 1680 and a labour force made up of African slaves soon formed the largest proportion of the population. Montserrat was one of the many coercive sugar and slave societies that European colonization of the Americas produced, beginning with Brazil in the mid-sixteenth century and arguably persisting to the present day in the sugar plantations of the Dominican Republic that are owned by foreign corporations and worked by unfree contract labourers from Haiti. These societies have burgeoned and faded as the world economy has changed and the land has become exhausted. But whatever their dates and locations over the last four centuries, their social correlates are the same and well-known: stratification and inequality; environmental degradation; the formation of peasantries and rural proletariats in the post-plantation period; and persisting problems with economic expansion, poverty, employment and education, whether or not these former colonies have achieved political independence.

Let us see whether, and how, these general features of the plantation economy have been played out in Montserrat. The British slave trade ended in 1807, and slavery itself was abolished and all slaves emancipated in the British colonies in 1834. Following emancipation was the period of what is called apprenticeship, when nominally free former slaves could be legally required to do work for their former masters for forty hours a week for four years. Montserratian landowners eagerly embraced the apprenticeship system; consequently, the condition of freed slaves in Montserrat was among the worst in the British Caribbean. Masters also devised other techniques for retaining the labour of their former slaves, among which was a system that required people to work in return for the privilege of cultivating a plot and occupying a house on land they did not own. This 'tenancy-at-will' could be terminated by the landowner at any time. Sharecroppping systems also developed. In any event, the freed people of Montserrat had less opportunity to acquire land of their own than did the people of some other British territories in the Caribbean. In Antigua, for example, apprenticeship was bypassed altogether.

In the latter half of the nineteenth century some black families were able to acquire land for houses and for cultivation under outright ownership, as plantations and estates began to break up. A few others could cultivate the island's unoccupied and crown lands as squatters. This was the beginning of a peasantry in Montserrat. However, for a large number of people the only recourse was emigration, as it was for many people throughout the Caribbean and as it is today. Montserrat has been seen as a prototypical emigration society; that is, a society in which the emigration of large numbers of people, and especially young people, took place so as to ensure the survival of the society as a whole, and was not just a strategy which ensured that the emigrants could survive. Thus two important and complementary developments in Montserratian history and society characterize the latter half of the nineteenth century: the growth of a peasantry, and the emergence of a migration pattern. These are complementary, as they are elsewhere in the world, since the peasant economy, carried out on marginal land for subsistence and for small amounts of money from the sale of cash crops, can not grow at the rate of the peasant population. The population must be kept in balance with resources, and since neither resources nor the economy expand, the population must be stabilized by the export of its young people. This economic and ecological necessity has become a part of Montserratian culture and values, so that migration becomes a desirable goal that young people strive to attain. The compulsion to send money back home to the family on the island has also been incorporated into the culture and into the social arrangements of émigré communities, where social pressure often succeeds in correcting remittance backsliders.

By the beginning of the twentieth century, Montserratian sugar production was about dead and the agricultural schemes of the previous half century, or so, that had been intended to replace it had also failed. These failed schemes included commercial lime production, which was destroyed by a hurricane in 1899, and an earlier scheme for raising silkworms that never flourished. Cotton production was being promoted in the British islands during the first twenty years of the century, and sea island cotton became an important agricultural export crop in Montserrat up until the 1950s. The decline of sea island cotton – a high quality, relatively expensive long staple variety – was linked to a decline in world demand as fashion dictated synthetic fabrics in the 1960s. Since 1968, Montserrat has had no widely grown, characteristic, and dependable world export crop. Cotton became a small specialty crop grown solely for a government-sponsored textile workshop where local weavers produce on a small scale for the tourist market. In the past two years, there have been some signs of a sea island cotton resuscitation. A regional cotton corporation that includes Montserrat has been formed and has built a central ginnery in Barbados in response to a growing market for this superior fibre.

At present, the principal problems that many Montserratians struggle with are how to secure economic expansion, and how to retain dependent political status as a British colony. Perhaps there is some hope for the new cotton scheme, but for the moment it appears that Montserrat has taken the low road – most likely a dead-end – to tourist development. Montserrat's kind of tourism reinforces the dependency state of mind and may forestall political independence indefinitely.

Contemporary Montserrat

During the 1960s, Montserrat was promoted in England and North America as an idyllic place to either retire, or to build a second house. Part of that idyll was, of course, that Montserrat was still a colony without an independence movement, and was consequently safe for this kind of individual investment by foreigners. Montserrat's tourism became 'residential tourism'. Land sales increased and the building trades expanded, boosting the economy temporarily, but threatening the availability of land for houses and for cultivation by Montserratians. Fortunately, the government restricted land aliena-tion and confined the building of foreign residences to designated parts of the island, so that land prices would not be distorted everywhere. The result is a ghetto of prosperous white foreigners, many of whom have a genuine interest in the island as well as in their own investment, and work toward enhancing amenities such as a museum and a preservation trust. These residents, however, and those who cater for them, make up a conservative core of resistance to political independence.

The land and building boom in Montserrat had ended by the early 1980s, but Montserrat received another economic boost with the establishment and operation of an offshore medical school catering for North Americans. This can be seen as another form of residential tourism. The medical students change, but the body of foreign residents remains dependable. In the 1980s, Montserrat also began an attempt to lure the transient tourist onto the island, and indeed transient visitor numbers have increased. It is well-known, however, that tourism does not always fulfil development goals, even while it expands. In most regions dependent on foreign tourism, only a tenth of the money that tourists spend remains in the local area, and it is questionable whether this tenth compensates for the local govern-mental investment in infrastructure, the environmental and resource burden, or the resentment of local people. The money does not remain in the locale because the large tourist facilities are not usually locally-owned and because the kinds of amenities that tourists require must usually be imported. It remains to be seen whether Montserrat can escape this pattern in its transient tourism development. However, it should be noted that some of Montserrat's tourist hotels are locally owned.

The second important issue is political status, and from some points of view Montserrat has recently been pushed a step backward. For most of its history Montserrat has been a legislative colony, a position it still retains. This means that it has had its own locally-elected government, although there has long been a resident governor who, for the most part, has been more a British crown representative on the island than the wielder of governmental authority. Montserrat has received many benefits from its status as a colony. It has had good hospital facilities and is included in Britain's national health plan. Emigrants to Britain have not had immigration problems. Montserrat also receives budget allocations. Understandably, then, many Montserratians prefer to remain a British dependent territory than to risk the unknowns of an independent statehood founded on limited resources.

As a dependent territory, Montserrat enjoyed, at least until recently, full self-government in internal affairs. The governor is an appointee who presides over Montserrat's executive council but did not until recently exercise authority. In 1989, however, the United Kingdom decided unilaterally to revise the constitution in ways that grant genuine power to the governor. These provisions went into effect in February, 1990, and were greatly resented. The Organization of Eastern Caribbean States strongly protested against the new provisions and powers, as did the Montserratian government. As a result, one of the governor's new powers was cancelled: the governor may not instigate legislation unless it has been approved by Montserrat's Legislative Council.

This step backward to colonial control was a consequence of problems in Montserrat's offshore banking industry that came to light in 1989. The international transactions of at least 300 offshore banks had supplied revenue to Montserrat amounting to more than a million East Caribbean dollars every year (in 1990 one hundred EC dollars equalled about thirty-seven US dollars and about twenty-one British pounds), but evidence of international fraud and money-laundering on the part of the banks led to the collapse of the industry in the summer of 1989.

Now that offshore banking is gone, the economic priorities of the present government continue to be the development of light industry and commercial agriculture, especially sea island cotton. In 1989, the islands of Montserrat, Antigua, and Barbados formed a company for the growing and marketing of this superior long staple cotton, and acquired a mill in Barbados to handle the product of the three islands. Montserrat's agricultural history is marked by the repeated failure and resuscitation of the sea island cotton industry, but this inter-island cooperative venture is an innovation that may succeed as the world market for very high quality cotton improves.

If it is not successful, the economy will remain dominated by service industries, and especially tourism, which makes up a quarter of the Gross Domestic Product. It is true that nearly three-quarters of the value of exports from the island comes from the products of light industries and that, in addition, Montserrat is a regional media centre. International recording studios are located there, and Radio Antilles, broadcasting to the Antillean region, is located in Montserrat. Nevertheless, the trade deficit amounted to about US$24,000,000 in 1988, a deficit balanced only by the remittances of émigrés living abroad and by the incomes of foreign expatriates living on the island.

Both of Montserrat's effective political parties have stated their commitment to agricultural development, to education, and to projects designed to improve infrastructure in order to open the way for other forms of economic development. The two parties are the Progressive Democratic Party (PDP) and the Peoples' Liberation Movement (PLM). In 1987, the PLM was returned to office for the third time. John Osborne, the PLM leader, is among the Montserratians who favour independent statehood. The PLM had planned a referendum on the independence issue, but the hurricane strike of 1989 that devastated the island obliterated all issues except recovery, for which aid from the United Kingdom has been essential.

Hurricane Hugo of 1989 struck Montserrat harder than any other Antillean island. Between the 17th and 19th of September, about ninety-five per cent of all buildings on the island, including the hospital, schools, churches, government structures, and tourist facilities, were completely, or partly, destroyed. Of 12,000 inhabitants, barely 120 were left with dwellings intact, and four people died. The airport continued to operate, but the harbour jetty was ruined and a week later, most of the population was still without running water. Radio Antilles anticipated being silent for up to six months and the total damage was estimated at EC$330,000,000.

Chief Minister Osborne expected Montserrat to be desperately crippled for years. Notwithstanding this, aid for reconstruction immediately followed the emergency relief provided by United Kingdom, and Montserrat has begun to rebuild and to restore itself more quickly than first anticipated.

Population and Infrastructure

About 12,000 people inhabit Montserrat's 38 square miles (98 square kilometres). This figure represents a drop of about 2,000 since 1960, and indicates not that deaths exceed births, but that out-migration is a significant element in Montserrat's demographic processes. Even so, the population density is about 316 per square mile (122.5 per square kilometre). The population growth rate is 0.6 per cent annually, and life expectancy at birth is 70.2 years. The land has suffered erosion and exhaustion in the past, the economy cannot accommodate everyone who would like a paid job, and emigration is the means by which the population is enabled to live above a subsistence level, even though small plot cultivation for subsistence and some cash is one important source of support for many households.

Montserrat's population is, like that of the other islands of the old Leeward Islands Colony, mostly descended from slaves of African origin. Moreover, like the populations of her sister islands, Montserrat's is stratified by class and colour, but without a native-born or creole white élite. Today's prosperous whites are all resident foreigners who have arrived since the 1960s. Over three-quarters of the native-born population is literate, and almost all are diglossic; that is, everyone speaks standard English as learned in school as well as Montserrat Creole, the local variety of the dialect mother tongue spoken everywhere in the formerly British Caribbean.

Plymouth is the principal town and the port for the island. Although the natural harbour at Plymouth is not very sheltered, it has been modified to create an anchorage of about 7.3 metres (24 feet) deep. Further improvements to the harbour were set back by Hurricane Hugo. There are about 203 kilometres (126 miles) of paved roads on the island, and 66 kilometres (412 miles) of dirt roads. The most recent improvement in road transport was the building of a coastal road on the east side of the island from Plymouth to Blackburne Airport. Electricity, piped water, health care, and public education are universal in the island, and there is also an extra-mural centre of the University of the West Indies.

Research on Montserrat

Research on Montserrat has been very much skewed in some directions, and abysmally lacking in others. Of all the natural sciences, research in geology predominates, and this research has been largely focused on the volcanic and seismic features of the island. Indeed, the attention given to Montserrat's volcanic and seismic activity has been obsessive. Perhaps this is understandable, since there are always active fumaroles and noticeable periods of elevated seismic activity, as in the 1930s and 1960s. However, there has been no eruption in historic times, and no earthquake since the seventeenth century.

There has also been a great deal of research carried out in the areas of agriculture and soils, most of it of an applied nature. This too is understandable, since agriculture has been Montserrat's main economic activity and interest in developing agriculture commercially has been intense and assiduous if only rarely productive. There has been little research in other applied and natural sciences, with the exception of some accomplishments in health and medicine, botany, ornithology, and a few areas of zoology. Montserrat is open territory for many areas of research, and desperately needs modern studies in ecology and biogeography, a detailed and specific study of plant communities, and thorough studies of marine and land animal species.

In the area of human sciences there has been some good contemporary research in history, historical geography, and archaeology (see works by Riva Berleant-Schiller, Conrad Goodwin, Lydia Pulsipher, and David Watters). In social and cultural anthropology there are only two major monographs, Jay Dobbins's work on Montserratian folk religion and Stuart Philpott's on the social anthropology of Montserrat as a migration society. Both books are good and tell us quite a lot about Montserratian society and culture in addition to their stated foci, but there is room for much more anthropological research. Yolanda Moses's work on the status of women now needs to be supplemented by modern work on gender and household. The work of Rhoda Métraux and Theodora Abel on psychological anthropology is limited and outdated, and there is still a great deal of room for research on cultural topics. John Messenger's work on the Irish influence in Montserrat cannot be accepted as a serious study of culture and history, but it suggests interesting research questions about ethnicity and identity. Even though Philpott has written about a migration society, we need to know more about the migration experiences of those involved. We would also benefit from a complete linguistic study of Montserrat Creole and Montserratian speech, as we would for most of the small islands of the Caribbean.

Riva Berleant-Schiller and Lydia Pulsipher have illuminated Montserrat in the seventeenth century and Douglas Hall has written about Montserrat after emancipation, but many more studies of Montserrat's social history are needed.

One Montserratian writer and historian, Howard Fergus, has enlightened us on many Montserrat topics related to politics and history. He is clearly attached to his island, but never lets his attachment muffle his critical faculties or blear his sharp eye for hypocrisy and nonsense. He is a forthright advocate for political independence, which will probably once more become a significant issue as the island continues to recover from Hurricane Hugo.

The Bibliography

This bibliography reflects the way in which research on Montserrat has been skewed. The sections on geology, natural hazards (i.e., hurricanes, earthquakes, and volcanoes) and agriculture are large, representing the substantial body of literature and great research efforts in these directions. Some areas are scanty, and we can only hope that this bibliography will help to make the research gaps more obvious. Some sections, such as history and periodicals, are extensive because there is a large regional literature that applies to, or includes, Montserrat, even though it does not focus exclusively on Montserrat.

In choosing materials for this bibliography I have worked according to several principles. I erred on the side of inclusion rather than selection, because the total literature is scanty by comparison to many other countries and territories. Indeed it is so scanty that many important subjects are almost totally left out, such as labour and employment, or foreign relations (although there are index references to these topics). Therefore, although I cannot say that this is a definitive bibliography of Montserrat, it *is* a widely inclusive one.

Where newspaper articles were the only available sources for topics which I considered to be important, I did not hesitate to use them. This was the case, for example, in covering Hurricane Hugo, the most recent cotton development, and the banking frauds of 1989. A more permanent literature will doubtless develop on these topics, but it has not yet emerged. I have also cited the reports of governmental and quasi-governmental bodies, as these were sometimes the only sources of information available on certain subjects. Because the bibliography tends to be inclusive, it clearly demonstrates the gaps in the literature and the areas where research is desperately needed.

Another principle I followed was that of including works on the Caribbean region, or on the Leeward Islands, where these either focused on topics significant to Montserrat, or included information about Montserrat. An example of this kind of material is Noel Deerr's monumental history of sugar, which both includes statistics on Montserratian sugar production in the eighteenth century which are not easily available elsewhere and provides an economic and historical context for Montserrat's period as a sugar island. Another example of this kind of work is Sidney Mintz's *Caribbean Transformations*, which is of fundamental importance to anybody wishing to gain any understanding of the region.

The entries in each section and subsection are arranged alphabetically by title. All of the entries are informative, but in selected cases they are also critical. There should be almost nothing in this bibliography that the dedicated researcher cannot find, no matter what his or her location. I was able to read most items by using interlibrary loan services. For those located near New York City, the Research Institute for the Study of Man is an invaluable resource. In London, I found many of the publications included here in the British Library, the library of the Institute of Commonwealth Studies, and the Royal Commonwealth Society library. Anyone who is interested in Montserrat or her neighbouring islands should follow the *Bulletin of Eastern Caribbean Affairs* and its back issues.

I am grateful to all those libraries and institutions where I have pursued my Caribbean researches, but I want especially to mention the library where I teach – the University of Connecticut at Torrington. Without the inexhaustible interlibrary loan services that our librarian Johanna Burkhardt extended I could not have put this bibliography together. Thanks also to Arnold Berleant and David Watters.

Riva Berleant-Schiller
Goshen, Connecticut, USA
June 1991

The Country and Its People

1 **Alliouagana in focus.**
J. A. George Irish. Plymouth, Montserrat: Montserrat Printery, 1973.
28p.
This short pamphlet tries to describe contemporary Montserrat and Montserratian culture realistically, without the myths and embellishments designed for tourists. The author, a native Montserratian, rightly emphasizes the West Indian nature of Montserrat's people and culture, even though many outsiders have tried to establish Irish sources and identify Irish traits. *Alliouagana* is said to be the name given to the island by its original Carib inhabitants.

2 **Country profile: Montserrat.**
Caricom Perspective, no. 36 (July-December 1986), p. 34-39.
This brief outline of Montserratian geography, history, economy, educational system and recent politics includes a description of Montserrat technical college and a biographical sketch of the chief minister in 1986, John Alfred Osborne.

3 **Data atlas for Montserrat.**
Eastern Caribbean Natural Area Management Programme, Caribbean Conservation Association, and School of Natural Resources of the University of Michigan. Christiansted, US Virgin Islands: ECNAMP, 1982.
This survey of Montserrat is part of a series that covers each island of the Lesser Antilles. Based on secondary sources, the pamphlet includes information on rainfall, land use, population density, watersheds, marine resources, transport and tourist attractions. It is illustrated with single-colour maps, and is available for US$2.00 from ECNAMP, P.P. Box 4010, Christiansted, USVI, 00820, USA.

1

4 *Financial Times* **survey: Montserrat.**

Raymond Whitaker. *Financial Times*, 29 May, 1980, p. 25.

This is an introductory survey of political and economic conditions in Montserrat, including a discussion of Montserrat's colonial relationship to Great Britain and the economic role of the offshore medical school that opened there in 1980.

5 **Montserrat and Montserratians.**

Hodge Kirnon. New York: The Author, 1925. 27p.

The author, a Montserratian living in New York, has written a short history of Montserrat specifically from the point of view of one who was born and reared there.

6 **Montserrat, B.W.I.: some implications of suspended culture change.**

Rhoda Métraux. *Transactions of the New York Academy of Sciences*, series II, vol. 20, no. 2 (1957), p. 205-11.

The author of this impressionistic essay spent eleven months in a rural Montserrat village in 1953-54. She argues that much of Montserratian belief and behaviour emanates from a preoccupation with slow but inexorable change. The value of the paper now lies in its description of rural life in the 1950s.

7 **Montserrat: emerald isle of the Caribbean.**

Howard A. Fergus. London: Macmillan, 1983. 86p. map. bibliog.

This is a general introduction to the island, illustrated with colour photographs, that will serve as a handbook for visitors and those working in the tourist industry. Topics covered include plants, animals, history, geography, folk culture, and things to do. The list of selected readings is, however, random and sketchy.

8 **The region: a single eastern Caribbean country.**

Caribbean Update, January 1989, p. 3.

This article briefly summarizes the then current (1989) political, economic and social climate in Montserrat.

9 **West Indian migration: the Montserrat case.**

Stuart B. Philpott. London: Athlone Press; New York: Humanities Press, 1973. 210p. map. bibliog. (London School of Economics Monographs on Social Anthropology, 47).

The first full-length published monograph on the culture, social organization and economy of Montserrat, this volume is still useful and authoritative. The first chapter is an accurate summary of history and the environment; subsequent chapters on social organization and social structure are shaped around the theme of out-migration and its effects on Montserratian society. The volume includes a chapter on emigrants living in Britain and the ways in which they maintain their ties with the island. As a comprehensive account of Montserrat, this monograph has not yet been superseded, despite its specific theme of migration. It is based on the author's doctoral dissertation, 'Mass migration in Montserrat' (q.v.).

Geography

General and regional

10 **Die Britische Inseln über dem Winde (Kleine Antillen).** (The British
Leeward Islands of the Lesser Antilles).
Helmut Blume. *Erdkunde*, vol. 15 (1961), p. 265-87.
Blume's comprehensive analysis by means of maps, diagrams and tables shows the
distribution of agricultural land holdings in the Anglophone Lesser Antilles (including
Montserrat) and classifies them by their size, agricultural use and type of land tenure.
He finds three economic regions, each of which is differentiated into large plantation
holdings and small peasant holdings. This differentiation, he argues, is related to
physical environment.

11 **The Caribbean islands.**
Helmut Blume. London: Longman, 1974. 464p. maps.
This is the standard geography of the Caribbean region. Part I covers structure,
oceanography, climate, land forms, flora and fauna, the native American population,
demography and economic geography. Part II devotes separate chapters to islands and
island groups, covering aspects of their physical, historical, agricultural, and population
geography. Illustrations are included.

12 **Commercial geography of Montserrat.**
Otis P. Starkey. Bloomington, Indiana: Indiana University
Department of Geography, 1960. 18p. maps. bibliog. (Technical Reports
on the Commercial Geography of British Islands in the Lesser Antilles,
no. 6).
This pamphlet reports on Montserrat's trade, infrastructure and production, including
export crops, livestock, forestry, quarrying, construction, services and manufacturing.
There are very brief sections on population, physiography and land tenure.

13 **Land settlement as an imposed solution.**
Janet Momsen. In: *Land and development in the Caribbean.* Edited
by Jean Besson, Janet Momsen. London: Macmillan Caribbean, 1987,
p. 46-69.
This paper examines the role of government in satisfying the need for land among the
rural small plot cultivators of the formerly British Caribbean. The author discusses
Montserrat briefly, in relation to schemes such as are described in *A land use plan for
Trants Estate, Montserrat* (q.v.) and *The new Otway farms: a land use plan for the
Otway Estate, Montserrat* (q.v.).

14 **Ridged fields in Montserrat, West Indies.**
Lydia Mihelic Pulsipher. *Proceedings of the Middle States Division of
the Association of American Geographers*, vol. 12 (1978), p. 77-80.
Montserratian cultivators hoe horizontal raised ridges across their fields, even when the
fields do not lie on slopes. The island landscape is marked by relict ridges in places that
are not currently under cultivation. The author discusses the functions of the ridges
and their possible cultural and historical origins.

Historical

15 **Assessing the usefulness of a cartographic curiosity: the map of a sugar
island.**
Lydia Mihelic Pulsipher. *Annals of the Association of American
Geographers*, vol. 77, no. 3 (1987), p. 408-22.
William Stapleton, second governor of the Leeward Islands, had a coastal profile map
drawn in 1673, *Mountserrat Island* (q.v.). This map shows the island as seen from
offshore on all sides, and includes cultural features such as houses, cultivation plots,
etc. From her study of the map and her research on the island Pulsipher concludes that
the map is an accurate representation of the island as it appeared in 1673.

16 **The cultural landscape of Montserrat in the seventeenth century: the
environmental effects of early British colonial development in the
Caribbean.**
Lydia Mihelic Pulsipher. PhD thesis, Southern Illinois University,
1977. 183p. (Available from University Microfilms, Ann Arbor,
Michigan, USA, 48106).
This is an earlier and longer version of the author's *Seventeenth-century Montserrat: an
environmental impact statement* (q.v.).

17   **English, Irish and African influences on the landscape of seventeenth-
      century Montserrat, West Indies.**
      Lydia Mihelic Pulsipher.   *Proceedings of the Middle States Division of
      the Association of American Geographers*, vol. 13 (1979), p. 5-8.
      The author summarizes the ways in which the English, Irish and African inhabitants of
      Montserrat in the seventeenth century brought their different cultural practices to bear
      on the landscape of the island.

18   **The historical record of man as an ecological dominant in the Lesser
      Antilles.**
      Gordon C. Merrill.   *Canadian Geographer*, vol. 11 (1958), p. 17-22.
      This article is a brief summary of the history of human-land relations in the Lesser
      Antilles, including Montserrat.

19   **Seventeenth century Montserrat: an environmental impact statement.**
      Lydia Mihelic Pulsipher.   Norwich, England: Geo Books, 1986. 96p.
      maps. bibliog. (Historical Geography Research Series, no. 17).
      A study of the environmental effects of English colonization, and the cultural
      landscape that developed as a consequence of colonial activities during the 1670s,
      especially tobacco and sugar production. The author examines the effects of colonial
      building, clearing, road-making, domestic animals and economic plants on the island
      and its vegetation, arguing that culture rather than nature is the primary influence on
      land use and human-land relationships. The study is based on field research and on the
      use of contemporaneous archival, census and map sources.

20   **The West Indies: patterns of development, culture and environmental
      change since 1492.**
      David Watts.   Cambridge, England: Cambridge University Press, 1987.
      609p. maps.
      The author has provided a comprehensive and definitive survey of the historical
      geography of the West Indies. One chapter is devoted to aboriginal population and
      land use, but the rest of the book deals with the region since 1492, when the European
      invasion instigated a history of overwhelming environmental and population change.
      There are many references to Montserrat.

Maps

21   **Lesser Antilles: Montserrat with Redonda.**
      Great Britain: Directorate of Overseas Surveys, 1967. Scale: 1:25,000.
      This colour transverse Mercator projection is one of a uniform Lesser Antilles series
      (DOS 359, series E803). It measures 57x77 cm., shows the small uninhabited island of
      Redonda, and was the base map for the *Tourist map of Montserrat* (q.v.).

22 **Map of Montserrat.**
Great Britain: Directorate of Overseas Surveys, 1962. Scale: 1:50,000.
This colour map, measuring 30x37 cm, includes a location map and shows relief by gradient tints and spot heights. It is the authoritative single-sheet map. A newer DOS multiple-sheet 1:10,000 map is in progress, but has not yet been completed.

23 **Mountserrat Island.**
Manuscript map. John Carter Brown Library, Brown University, Providence, Rhode Island, 1673. Unscaled.
This unusual coastal profile map is part of the *Blathwayt Atlas*, a collection compiled by William Blathwayt for England's Committee of the Lords of Trade and Plantations in 1673. It shows the important physical and cultural features of the island at that time. The *Blathwayt Atlas* has been published in facsimile form, so that the map is available for study (Jeannette Black, [ed.], Brown University Press, 2 vols., 1970 and 1975).

24 **Tourist map of Montserrat.**
Great Britain: Directorate of Overseas Surveys, 1983. Scale: 1:25,000.
This colour transverse Mercator projection, measuring 72x78 cm., shows relief by contours, gradient tints and spot heights. It includes an inset map of the principal town, Plymouth, on a scale of 1:5,000. The entire map shows parish boundaries and includes a written description of Montserrat and an index to buildings in Plymouth. It is based on the DOS 1:25,000 map of 1967 (q.v.).

Data atlas for Montserrat.
See item no. 3.

Caribbean Conservation News.
See item no. 316.

Caribbean Geography.
See item no. 320.

Tourism and Travel

Tourism

25 **The Caribbean's emerald isle.**
Stephen Knox. *Caribbean and West Indies Chronicle*, vol. 99, no. 9
(Feb.-Mar. 1983), p. ii-iv.
This is an excellent example of the tourist- and investor-oriented brief survey that
completely ignores the culture and social and economic realities of Caribbean daily
life. It promotes uncritically the myth of Montserratian Irishness and describes
Montserrat from the perspective of a leisured tourist. The best illustration of its bland,
superficial character is found in the list of key dates in Montserrat's history, in which
1834, the year of slave emancipation in Montserrat and throughout the British
colonies, is omitted!

26 **The happy homesteaders of Montserrat.**
James Ramsey Ullman. *Caribbean Beachcomber*, vol. 4, no. 4 (July-
Aug. 1968), p. 13-15.
Ullman's 'happy homesteaders' are in fact prosperous North American and British
expatriates who find it pleasant and economically advantageous to build houses and
settle in Montserrat. This article is written from their point of view for a readership of
similar, potential expatriates.

27 **Montserrat: a $33.5 million hotel.**
Caribbean Update, (March 1989), p. 13.
This article describes plans for a new hotel in Montserrat, to be built as individual
villas and sold as condominium units.

28   **Montserrat Island is on comeback after severe damage from Hugo.**
     Travel Agent Magazine, (6 Nov. 1989), p. 87.
Less than two months after hurricane Hugo devastated Montserrat, the Montserrat tourism bureau explained how the island was recovering quickly from a tourism standpoint.

29   **Montserrat: the way the Caribbean used to be.**
     Peter A. Dickinson.   *Wealth*, vol. 1, no.1 (1983), p. 28-30.
This article touts Montserrat as a 'retirement Eden', where North American expatriates can retire to live cheaply and luxuriously in a balmy location that offers good business and investment possibilities and low taxes. It is a perfect example of the kind of appeal to resident tourism that Howard A. Fergus criticizes so acutely in *Montserrat: paradise or prison?* (q.v.).

30   **Montserrat: visitor arrivals.**
     Caribbean Update, (September 1989), p. 15.
The tourism receipts in Montserrat increased to $29.2 million in East Caribbean currency in 1988, from an estimated EC$25.3 million in 1987.

31   **Regional report no. 15: the organization of East Caribbean states.**
     Economist Intelligence Unit.   *International Tourism Quarterly*, no. 1
     (1985), p. 30-39.
This report on the tourism sector of the economies and the tourism potential of each of the eight members of the Organization of East Caribbean States includes a discussion of Montserrat. Montserrat is not a major tourist destination, although potential for further tourism development exists. An airfield capable of handling large jets is recommended.

Travellers' accounts

32   **Behold the West Indies.**
     Amy Oakley.   New York: Appleton-Century, 1941. 540p.
The author travelled through the Caribbean in 1939 and 1940. Her account is an excellent example of stereotyped perceptions of the region and a demonstration of the ways such perceptions are fostered and circulated. The text is enlivened by black-and-white illustrations by Thornton Oakley that do exhibit a sense of place. Montserrat occupies pages 270-74.

33   **Love and the Caribbean.**
     Alec Waugh.   New York: Farrar, Straus, & Cudahy, 1958. 310p.
In his section on Montserrat, Waugh calls Montserrat 'one of the loveliest islands in my experience' (p. 29), and describes its mountains, valleys, volcanic craters and old windmills.

34 **Outposts: journeys to the surviving relics of the British Empire.**
Simon Winchester. London: Hodder & Stoughton, 1986. 360p.
As the title suggests, the author journeyed to the few remaining colonial territories of
Great Britain, and his book includes an account of contemporary Montserrat.

35 **Six months in the West Indies in 1825.**
Henry Nelson Coleridge. New York: Carvill, Bliss & White, 1826.
326p.
Coleridge travelled by sloop through the West Indies as secretary to his uncle, who was
the Anglican bishop of the Leeward Islands Colony. They stopped at Montserrat,
where Coleridge saw and described more of the local life on the island than most
casual visitors do. His lively account is far from complete, but exposes some aspects of
island life before emancipation.

36 **The West Indies in 1837.**
Joseph Sturge, Thomas Harvey. London: Hamilton, Adams & Co.,
1838. Reprinted, London: Frank Cass 1968. 476p.
The authors travelled through the British West Indies to report on the condition of
former slaves during apprenticeship, the period following emancipation when, by
British law, they could be required to work 45 hours each week on sugar estates in
return for food, housing and clothing. The section on Montserrat (p. 81-89) describes
people the authors met, includes observations on education and religion (both of which
they found in a sorry state), and reports on the resistance of some planters to full
emancipation. The authors emphasize the dangers of apprenticeship to the ultimate
freedom of former slaves, and the deteriorating social and political conditions on the
island, where incompetent and corrupt officials and governing bodies acted solely out
of personal interest.

Travel guides

37 **Birnbaum's Caribbean.**
Stephen Birnbaum. New York: Houghton-Mifflin, 1991. 975p. maps.
This is a general guide to the Caribbean Islands that appears annually. It supplements
the ordinary information on tourist facilities with material on history, language, politics
and the people.

38 **A cruising guide to the Lesser Antilles.**
Donald M. Street, Jr. New York: Dodd & Mead, 1966. 242p. maps.
This is the standard guide for those sailing in the waters of the Lesser Antilles, and
thus focuses mainly on the waters surrounding Montserrat and on possible anchorages,
which are apparently few and unsatisfactory. What it does say about the island is
superficial, and emanates from the point of view of prosperous North American
tourists (p. 191-95). Illustrations are included.

39 **Fielding's Caribbean.**
    Margaret Zellers. New York: William Morrow & Co., 1991. 876p.
    map.
This is a standard guide that includes information on hotels, restaurants, sports, sightseeing, medical facilities, outward appearances, and other categories of conventional tourist interest. The 1991 edition includes some interesting observations on the recovery from hurricane Hugo in 1989. It otherwise presents a rather superficial view of Montserrat.

40 **Fodor's Caribbean.**
    Fodor Travel. New York: Fodor Travel Publications, 1991. 645p.
    maps.
Of the three guides listed here, this one has the most information on hotels, food and sightseeing packed into the fewest pages. It has the least information on matters relating to history and culture.

Montserrat: emerald isle of the Caribbean
See item no. 7.

Tourist map of Montserrat.
See item no. 24.

Agriculture and tourism essential.
See item no. 216.

Development plan, 1966-1970.
See item no. 218.

Report on prices, trade, and tourism.
See item no. 306.

Tourism report.
See item no. 307.

Caribbean tourism statistical report.
See item no. 327.

Geology

General and regional

41 **Beiträge zur regionalen Geologie der Erde. Vol. 4: Geologie der Antillen.**
(Contributions to the regional geology of the earth. Vol. 4: geology of
the Antilles.)
R. Weyl. Berlin: Gebrüder Borntraeger, 1966. 410p. maps. bibliog.
A comprehensive geology of the Lesser and Greater Antilles that includes Montserrat
and its geological relationships to the rest of the Lesser Antillean chain. The volcanic
geology and petrology of Montserrat are described on p. 197-99.

42 **The formation of the Lesser Antilles.**
W. M. Davis. *Proceedings of the National Academy of Science*, vol. 10,
no. 6 (15 June, 1924), p. 205-11.
This article summarizes the development of the banks, reefs, atolls and volcanic cones
that constitute the Lesser Antillean arc. Montserrat is described as formed by a
mature, dissected volcanic cone of probable Pliocene age that has been augmented by
much younger cones on its southern side and adjoined on its northern side by an ocean
bank (p. 209).

43 **The geology of Montserrat, British West Indies.**
John W. Rea. PhD thesis, University of Oxford, 1970. 388p. maps.
bibliog.
A full-length study of Montserrat's geology that refines the earlier work of MacGregor
(q.v.) by the application of innovative methods unknown in MacGregor's time. The
sequence of eruptions, the relative ages of volcanic centres, and their geological
relations to each other are clarified and defined.

Geology. General and regional

44 **The geology of Saba and St. Eustatius, with notes on the geology of St. Kitts, Nevis, and Montserrat.**
J. H. Westermann, H. Kiel. Curaçao: Scientific Foundation of Surinam and the Netherlands Antilles, Publication 24. 1961. 175p. maps. bibliog.
Although Montserrat is not the major focus of this well-illustrated report, notes on the structure and volcanology of the island are included.

45 **Geophysical investigations in the Eastern Caribbean.**
C. B. Officer, J. I. Ewing, R. S. Edwards, H. R. Johnson. *Bulletin of the Geological Society of America*, vol. 68 (March 1957), p. 359-78.
This research explores the geological structure of the Venezuelan Basin underlying the Caribbean Sea, the Lesser Antilles, the Greater Antilles, and the Puerto Rico trench. The authors conclude that the tectonic activity that created the island arcs and deep-sea trenches was related to large and extensive intrusions of magma from deep in the earth's mantle.

46 **Gravity anomalies and island arc structure with particular reference to the West Indies.**
H. H. Hess. *Proceedings of the American Philosophical Society*, vol. 79, no. 1 (1938), p. 71-96.
This contribution to the structural geology of the Lesser Antilles and Caribbean Basin is based on undersea research done by the US Navy's Geophysical Union expedition of 1936-37. It relates gravity anomalies in the Caribbean Basin to the geologic structures and mountain-forming processes underlying the Lesser Antilles. Seismic and volcanic activity, notable in Montserrat, are partially correlated with negative gravity anomalies. The study demonstrates that the geological substructure of the Lesser Antilles forms a link between the east-west mountain ranges of the Greater Antilles and the east-west ranges of the Venezuelan Andes.

47 **Historical geology of the Antillean-Caribbean region.**
Charles Schuchert. New York: John Wiley & Sons; London: Chapman & Hall, 1935. 811p. bibliog.
The Caribbean arc of volcanic oceanic islands begins in the north with Saba, ends in the south with Grenada, and includes Montserrat. This volume is a valuable source of detailed information on the historical geology, structural geology and biogeography of the islands of this arc that allows the reader to understand the geology of Montserrat in its wider context. It includes a comprehensive bibliography to 1935.

48 **Holocene bioherms of the Lesser Antilles – geologic control of development.**
Walter H. Adey, Randolph B. Burke. In: *Reefs and related carbonates – ecology and sedimentology*. Edited by Stanley H. Frost, Malcolm P. Weiss, John B. Saunders. Tulsa, Oklahoma: American Association of Petroleum Geologists, 1977, p. 67-81. maps. bibliog.
On volcanic islands of the Lesser Antilles coral reefs become established only slowly, since volcanism and seismic activity lead to unstable shorelines. This is the case in Montserrat, where geologically recent volcanism and earthquakes discourage the

growth of large coral reefs. However, the longer the quiescence of volcanic and seismic activity, the larger the reef platforms. The resulting structures may themselves then be subject to subsidence, uplift, changes in sea level and even renewed volcanism.

49 The Lesser Antilles.
    W. M. Davis. New York: American Geographic Society, 1926. 207p. bibliog. (AGS Publication, 2).

Davis explains the volcanic, erosional and depositional processes that succeeded crustal deformation and sea floor subsidence and created the Lesser Antillean island chain. Montserrat, on the inner edge of the chain, belongs to the group of younger volcanic islands, which have not yet undergone the erosion and deposition that form the older, limestone islands of the outer edge.

50 Reports on the geology of the Leeward and British Virgin Islands.
    P. H. A. Martin-Kaye. Castries, St. Lucia: Voice Publishing Co., 1959. 117p. bibliog.

The author, formerly a British government geologist in the Caribbean colonies and later a United Nations geologist in Ethiopia, based his detailed works on intensive field research. His geological descriptions of the British Virgin and Leeward Islands include Montserrat and cover historical geology, volcanology, stratigraphy and surface features.

51 Royal Society expedition to Montserrat, B.W.I.: preliminary report on the geology of Montserrat.
    A. G. MacGregor. *Proceedings of the Royal Society of London*, Series B, vol. 121, no. B822 (1936), p. 232-52.

This preliminary account of Montserrat's geology is based on field work undertaken in 1936. It covers topography, relation of surface features to underlying structure, and volcanology. It lists and describes active *soufrières*.

52 A summary of the geology of the Lesser Antilles.
    P. H. A. Martin-Kaye. *Overseas Geology and Mineral Resources*, vol. 10, no. 2 (1969), p. 172-206.

This summary of the geological origin, orogenesis, structure and stratigraphy of the Lesser Antilles island chain includes a brief discussion of Montserrat (p. 192-93) and sets Montserrat in the structural and historical context of the entire Lesser Antillean region.

53 Stratification and circulation in the Antillean-Caribbean basins.
    Georg Wüst. New York; London: Columbia University Press, 1964. 2 vols. maps. bibliog.

This two-volume work constitutes a comprehensive description and mapping of the waters of the partially enclosed basins of the Antilles and Caribbean. It includes an analysis of their oxygen content, their circulation patterns, temperature, salinity and interaction with the atmosphere. These data were obtained from core samples taken by thirty-eight different research vessels from 1873 to 1961. Volume 1, the atlas volume, maps the distribution of such phenomena as precipitation, currents, water strata and salinity. A fold-out map of the Caribbean sea floor shows the underwater basin and mountain range formations and indicates their relation to the islands that break the surface of the sea.

Volcanology

54 **Andesites of the Lesser Antilles.**
John W. Rea. *Proceedings of the Geological Society of London*, no. 1662 (1970), p. 39-46.

Two kinds of lava have been extruded on the volcanic islands of the Lesser Antilles: basalt and andesite. This article discusses these volcanic islands, giving special attention to Montserrat, where andesites predominate and basalts are confined to South Soufrière Hill.

55 **Geochemistry and genesis of Lesser Antillean volcanic rocks.**
J. F. Tomblin. *Transactions of the 5th Caribbean Geological Conference* (1971), p. 153.

This is the brief abstract of a paper presented at the 5th Caribbean Geological Conference in 1971. The paper discusses the origin, distribution, and physical and chemical structure of Lesser Antillean volcanic rocks, including those of Montserrat.

56 **Geology of the southern part of Montserrat, West Indies.**
John W. Rea. *Proceedings of the Geological Society of London*, no. 1649, (1968), p. 115-16.

This note describes the volcanic geology and petrology of Montserrat's South Soufrière Hill, one of the most recent of the five major volcanic centres in Montserrat.

57 **A lava from Montserrat.**
Thomas Waller. *Geological Magazine*, n.s. decade II, vol. 10 (1883), p. 290-93.

A detailed description of the visual and physical properties of a hornblende andesite rock of volcanic origin from Montserrat.

58 **Montserrat and the West Indian volcanoes.**
Gerald Lenox-Conyngham. *Nature*, vol. 139, no. 5526 (1937), p. 907-10.

Montserrat was formed entirely by volcanic action, and today at least six distinct cones are identified, even though there has been no eruption since the first European sighting of the island in 1493. From about the end of 1933 to 1937, however, Montserrat experienced a period of continual and alarming earthquake rumbling, though no disaster occurred. This article discusses the seismic crisis and sets it in a comparative context of similar events and of theories concerning the geologic structure and processes of volcanic arcs.

59 **The relationship between andesitic volcanism and seismicity in Indonesia, the Lesser Antilles, and island arcs.**
T. Hatherton, W. R. Dickinson. *Journal of Geophysical Research*, vol. 74 (1969), p. 5301-10.

Information gathered from Montserrat contributes to this synthesizing research that explores the relationship between the potash content in lavas erupted from andesite volcanoes and the depth of their underlying seismic zone.

60 **The Royal Society expedition to Montserrat, B.W.I.: the volcanic history and petrology of Montserrat.**
A. G. MacGregor. *Philosophical Transactions of the Royal Society of London*, Series B, vol. 229, no. B557 (1939), p. 1-90. maps. bibliog.

This useful and detailed report is based on research prompted by the seismic and volcanic activity that Montserrat experienced in 1934 and 1935. It includes a review of the literature on the geology of the Lesser Antilles and of Montserrat; a summary of Montserrat's volcanic history; descriptive accounts of Montserrat's volcanic centres, fumaroles, hot springs, petrology and palaeontology; and a conclusion that attempts to interpret a pattern of volcanic events in the Lesser Antilles.

61 **The volcanic geology and petrology of Montserrat, West Indies.**
John W. Rea. *Journal of the Geological Society of London*, vol. 130, no. 4 (1974), p. 341-66.

This article is based on Rea's detailed re-examination of Montserrat's petrology and volcanic geology, a topic first researched by A. G. MacGregor in 1936 and 1939 (q.v.). Rea identified eight volcanoes on Montserrat, five of which he considered major centres, with three parasitic formations. The younger volcanoes are emphasized here. Using radiometric dating, a technique unavailable to MacGregor, Rea established their ages and the sequence of their eruptions.

Natural Hazards: Volcanic Eruptions, Earthquakes and Hurricanes

62 **An account of 'the sulphur' or 'soufrière' on the island of Montserrat.**
Nicholas Nugent. *Transactions of the Geological Society of London*,
vol. 1 (1811), p. 185-90.

This is one of the earliest descriptions of a fumarole on Montserrat. Even though
Nugent's visit to Galway's Soufrière in the southern part of the island took place in
1810, his description of the ascending mountain path, the small natural amphitheatre,
the absence of a definitive crater, and the surrounding peaks and vegetation still fits.

63 **Ein Besuch der Insel Montserrat** (A visit to the island of Montserrat.)
Karl Sapper. *Centralblatt der Mineralogie, Geologie, und
Palaeontologie*, 1903, p. 279-83.

Sapper visited two fumaroles in Montserrat in 1903, Galway's and Gage's, recording
their temperatures and mapping the main fumaroles at Galway's.

64 **Bibliography of the literature of the West Indian eruptions published in
the United States.**
E. O. Hovey. *Bulletin of the Geological Society of America*, vol. 15
(1904), p. 552-56.

This bibliography covers the US literature on the volcanic eruptions in the West Indies
up to 1903. It contains many references to the volcanic literature of Montserrat and the
West Indian region that are not included in this volume.

65 **Caribbean resort islands are hit by worst hurricane in a decade.**
Jeffrey Schmalz. *New York Times*, vol. 138 (September 18, 1989),
p. A1, A14.

This news report describes hurricane Hugo, which devastated Montserrat in
September, 1989, and destroyed nearly ninety-five per cent of houses and other
buildings.

66   Catalogue of the active volcanoes of the world including solfataric fields.
      Part XX, West Indies.
      G. R. Robson, J. F. Tomblin.   Rome: International Association of
      Volcanology, 1966. 28p. bibliog.
This catalogue provides descriptions of all of the active volcanoes and fumaroles in the
West Indies, including those of Montserrat.

67   An earthquake catalogue for the eastern Caribbean 1530-1960.
      G. R. Robson.   *Bulletin of the Seismological Society of America*, vol.
      54, no. 2 (1964), p. 785-832.
This is a list of all earthquakes recorded in the eastern Caribbean, including
Montserrat, from 1530 to 1960. Robson discovered twenty reports of seismic episodes
for Montserrat, beginning in 1690, some of which encompassed a time period of weeks
or months and included more than a single quake.

68   Hit hardest by hurricane, Montserrat starts to rebuild.
      John Kifner.   *New York Times*, vol. 139. (September 22, 1989), p. A12,
      A22.
This article reports on the immediate steps being taken to restore vital functioning and
to rebuild the island after Montserrat was struck by hurricane Hugo.

69   Hugo versus Montserrat.
      Edited by E. A. Markham, H. A. Fergus.   Plymouth, Montserrat:
      Coleraine & Boston, 1991. 108p.
I have been unable to obtain a copy of this publication which was being published just
as the manuscript of the present bibliography was being completed.

70   Major aid effort needed in wake of hurricane Hugo.
      Caribbean Insight, vol. 12, no. 10 (Oct. 1989), p. 1-2.
Hurricane Hugo devastated the eastern Caribbean between 17th and 19th September,
1989. Montserrat was the island most heavily damaged, with four deaths and an
estimated ninety-five per cent of all structures damaged or totally destroyed. This news
article outlines the worst consequences of the storm for Montserrat and nearby islands.

71   Mapping the volcanic hazards from Soufrière Hills volcano, Montserrat,
      West Indies, using an image processor.
      G. Wadge, M. C. Isaacs.   *Journal of the Geological Society*, vol. 145,
      part 4 (1988), p. 541-51.
Using a digital model of Montserrat's topography, a mathematical model of
gravitational flow and some educated assumptions about the development of volcanic
eruptions, the authors have mapped the probable consequences of a volcanic eruption
at Soufrière Hills. The map shows the areas most likely to be covered by lava flow in
the order that they would be affected during the successive stages of eruption. The
map is intended to be useful for emergency planning on the island.

72 **Montserrat: her disasters; a souvenir of the great hurricane of September 12th-13th, 1928.**
Fred E. Peters. New York: Steber Press, 1928. 51p.
The author sketches a brief history of the island and lists reported earthquakes, hurricanes and floods from 1775 to 1928. The hurricane of 1928 wiped out many landmarks, old houses, old trees, and two churches, St. Patrick's (Roman Catholic) and St. Anthony's (Anglican). The book is especially valuable for its photographs of Montserrat buildings and other features as they were before 1928.

73 **The Royal Society Expedition to Montserrat, B.W.I.: preliminary report on seismic observations.**
C. F. Powell. *Proceedings of the Royal Society of London*, series A, vol. 158, no. A894 (1937), p. 479-94.
This preliminary report is based on field observations of seismic activity that Powell made in Montserrat from 24th March to 24th July, 1936. Powell discovered that the shocks were local in origin and that activity reached its highest intensity in the earthquake of November 10, 1935, after three years of lesser shocks that were regularly concentrated between May and November.

74 **The Royal Society expedition to Montserrat, B.W.I.: final report.**
C. F. Powell. *Philosophical Transactions of the Royal Society of London*, series A, vol. 237, no. A771 (1938), p. 1-34.
This is the final authoritative report on the volcanic-seismic crisis that Montserrat experienced from 1933 to 1937. An expedition from the Royal Society installed instruments to measure and record seismic shocks. The report describes the instruments, analyses the data they recorded, and provides a general discussion of earthquake activity in the Lesser Antilles.

75 **Some heat measurements in West Indian soufrières.**
G. R. Robson, P. L. Willmore. *Bulletin Volcanologique*, vol. 17 (1955), p. 13-39.
Montserrat has, by most counts, seven active fumaroles, in which the intensity of heat production appears to be directly correlated with seismic activity. Robson and Willmore took measurements in Montserrat twenty years after a period of seismic activity, and discovered a sharp decline in heat output from measurements taken within a few years of the seismic crisis, as reported by Frank Perret in *The volcanic-seismic crisis at Montserrat 1933-1937* (q.v.).

76 **Volcanic eruptions in the West Indies.**
Longfield Smith. *West Indian Bulletin*, vol. 3 (1902), p. 271-93.
An account of the volcanic eruptions throughout the West Indies, including Montserrat, accompanied by observers' descriptions of the phenomena as they occurred, wherever such descriptions are available.

77 **The volcanic-seismic crisis at Montserrat 1933-1937.**
Frank A. Perret. *Carnegie Institution of Washington Publications*, no.
512 (1939).
Perret studied the fumarole known as Gage's Lower Soufrière during the volcanic-seismic crisis in Montserrat that lasted from 1933 to 1937, and measured the changes in its output of hydrogen sulphide.

78 **Volcano-seismic crisis in Montserrat, West Indies, 1966-67.**
J. B. Shepherd, J. F. Tomblin, D. A. Woo. *Bulletin Volcanologique*,
vol. 35, no. 1 (1971), p. 143-63.
In 1966 the Soufrière Hills volcano of southeastern Montserrat saw sharp increases in seismic and solfataric activity. Because this volcano erupted lava as recently as 1646 it is necessary to study and predict its behaviour. The authors determine the nature of the magma movements beneath the volcano and try to establish criteria for judging the probability of eruption in any future volcanic-seismic crises.

Montserrat Island is on comeback after severe damage from Hugo.
See item no. 28.

Fielding's Caribbean.
See item no. 39.

Horrors of a hurricane.
See item no. 287.

Flora and Fauna

Ecology and conservation

79　**Environmental guidelines for development in the Lesser Antilles.**
Technical report #3.
Eastern Caribbean Natural Area Management Programme.
Christiansted, US Virgin Islands: ECNAMP, 1984.
This report explains the ecological relationships and critical natural habitats common in
the Lesser Antilles, including Montserrat. Among the habitats and ecosystems that
should be protected are mangrove swamps, coral reefs, fishery resources, and human
cultural and ecological relationships.

80　**Fragments of paradise: a guide for conservation action in the U.K.**
dependent territories.
S. Oldfield.　Oxford: Pisces Publications, 1987. 192p.
This report considers the threats to the environment in the United Kingdom's
dependent territories, and the role of the British government in conservation. Part 2 is
made up of sections concerning each individual territory, including Montserrat, that
detail physical characteristics, economy, land use, flora and fauna, marine resources,
habitats and protected areas. Each section also includes an assessment of conservation
efforts and legislation, and recommendations for conservation.

81　**The Windward and Leeward Islands considered in relation to forestry.**
Francis Watts.　*West Indian Bulletin*, vol. 13 (1913), p. 293-314.
This paper shows that the importance of preserving forests in mountainous tropical
islands such as the Lesser Antilles was recognized early in this century. Forests are not
only economically useful; they are essential for maintaining water balance and
shielding slopes from erosion. Montserrat receives special attention in relation to the
destructive hurricane of 1899 and the need for establishing forest reserves on the island
(p. 305-07).

Plants

82 Agave in the West Indies.
William Trelease. *Memoirs of the National Academy of Sciences*, vol. 11 (1913), p. 4-95.

This article clarifies the structure, systematics and distribution of the fifty species of *Agave* found in the Caribbean Islands, and argues that the original parent stock was a North American species. *Agave montserratensis*, found only on Montserrat, is part of the larger group, *Agave karatto*, distributed throughout the Lesser Antilles (p. 24-29; plates B, 18 and 19).

83 An all yellow form of *Oncidium urophyllum*.
R. J. Midgett. *American Orchid Society Bulletin*, vol. 58, no. 2 (1989), p. 124-25.

A new form of the epiphyte *Oncidium urophyllum* was discovered in Montserrat in 1985 in dry woodland. Although the colouring of this species usually combines yellow with red-brown, the Montserrat orchid is entirely yellow and will be of great value for breeding purposes in horticulture.

84 Flowers of the Caribbean.
G. W. Lennox. London: Macmillan Caribbean, 1988. 72p.

This guide, illustrated in colour, will be useful for the non-botanist who wishes to identify and name the common flowering plants of the Caribbean.

85 Herbaceous angiosperms of the Lesser Antilles.
Ismael Vélez. San Juan: Biology Department, Inter-American University of Puerto Rico, 1957. 121p. bibliog.

The author collected and classified the herbaceous plants and plant communities of the Lesser Antilles. He includes grasses, flowering plants, cacti, climbers and woody shrubs, and arranges his discussion by types of environment in which different plant communities are found. A checklist indicates where in the Lesser Antilles each species is found. The book includes several photographs of Montserrat and provides the means for extracting a list of the island's herbaceous plants and shrubs.

86 Modern problems of the years 1492-1800 in the Lesser Antilles.
Richard A. Howard. *Annals of the Missouri Botanical Garden*, vol. 62, no. 2 (1975), p. 368-79.

Howard has compiled a history of the plant collections made in the Lesser Antilles, including Montserrat, and discusses the problems of taxonomy and of understanding distribution patterns that arise from the multiple discovery and naming of Lesser Antillean plants.

87 The natural vegetation of the Windward and Leeward Islands.
J. S. Beard. Oxford: Clarendon Press, 1949. 192p. maps. bibliog.

This is a seminal work, based entirely on field research, that has been supplemented but not superseded. It is a good introduction to the plant geography of the Windwards and Leewards, and to the human and physical environmental factors that influence the distribution of plant species throughout the islands. The author describes the plant communities on each island (Montserrat occupies pages 104-07), classifies the types of plant communities, and adds comparative studies of Trinidad, Tobago, Puerto Rico and Mauritius.

88 **Report on a visit to the island of Montserrat.**
J. A. Shafer. *New York Botanical Garden Journal*, vol. 8, no. 88 (1907), p. 81-88.

This brief report recapitulates five weeks spent investigating Montserratian plant communities and collecting specimens for the New York Botanical Garden. It reviews the common wild plants of the major environments in all parts of the island: beach, fumaroles, windward cliffs, moist slopes and mountain peaks, dry areas of the mountain rainshadow, freshwater ponds and eroded guts. A summary of economic plants is also included. This is the first botanical survey of the island, the only earlier plant collection having been made in 1802.

89 **Trees of the Caribbean.**
S. A. Seddon. London: Macmillan Caribbean, 1980. 88p.

This is an illustrated guide to the trees of the Caribbean. It is particularly useful for the non-specialist as an introduction to the subject.

90 **The vegetation of the Antilles.**
Richard A. Howard. In: *Vegetation and vegetational history of northern Latin America.* Edited by Alan Graham. Amsterdam; New York: Elsevier, 1973, p. 1-37.

This article classifies the types of vegetation in the Greater and Lesser Antilles and analyses their distribution, origin and relationships to climate and physical environment. It is especially useful for the study of Montserrat because it describes the kinds of ecological niches and associated plant genera that are found on the island, and allows one to understand Montserrat in its wider physical and biotic Antillean setting.

91 **Volcanism and vegetation in the Lesser Antilles.**
Richard A. Howard. *Journal of the Arnold Arboretum*, vol. 3, no. 3 (1962), p. 279-334.

Throughout the volcanic islands of the Lesser Antilles, including Montserrat, volcanism has influenced the plant communities. This article is based on the author's field trips to the Lesser Antilles and on an exhaustive review of the literature. He visited Montserrat in 1961, and paid special attention to the effects of fumaroles on plant life (p. 292-95; p. 301-04). The report includes several photographs of Montserrat's fumaroles and their surrounding vegetation.

92 **Why Montserrat?**
Richard A. Howard. In: *Leewards: writings, past and present, about the Leeward Islands.* Edited by John Brown. Bridgetown, Barbados: Department of Extra-Mural Studies, University College of the West Indies, 1961, p. 12-17.

This essay by a botanist explains the reasons why Montserrat has been such an excellent place for carrying out research, especially on the relationship of volcanic activity to vegetation.

Mammals

93   **First record of a *Monophyllus* from Montserrat, West Indies.**
     E. D. Pierson, W. E. Rainey, R. M. Warner, C. C. White-Warner.
     Mammalia, vol. 50, no. 2 (1986), p. 269-71.

This brief report records the first observation on Montserrat of the Lesser Antillean long-tongued bat, *Monophyllus plethodon*, known on several other of the larger islands of the Lesser Antilles.

Birds

94   **Aspects of the breeding biology of the cattle egret (*Bulbucus ibis*) in Montserrat West Indies, and its impact on nest vegetation.**
     W. J. Arendt, A. I. Arendt.   *Colonial Waterbirds*, vol. 11, no. 1 (1988), p. 72-84.

Montserrat provided an island environment for the study of the reproductive ecology of the cattle egret. The authors discovered that nest size was smaller than that of cattle egrets in other environments, probably because of scarce nesting materials. Consequently, average clutch size was also smaller. The authors hypothesize that because of interspecific competition for nesting materials, along with other environmental factors such as storms, grazing and woodcutting, the cattle egret is contributing to the decline of the small tidal mangrove ecosystem at Fox's Bay, Montserrat.

95   **Birds of Montserrat.**
     Alan Siegel.   Plymouth, Montserrat: Montserrat National Trust, 1983. 48p.

This is a brief illustrated account of the birds of Montserrat and serves as an introduction and a checklist for the bird-watcher on the island. It complements the classic *Birds of the West Indies* (q.v.).

96   **Birds of the West Indies.**
     James Bond.   London: Collins, 1971. 256p. maps.

This is the only complete handbook to the birds of the West Indies. Every species known to the region is described, with either a black-and-white or colour illustration, local and scientific names, and information on nesting, habitat, vocalizations, range and migration. The book is intended mainly for field identification and quick reference.

97   **A general catalog of the birds of the Lesser Antilles.**
     George N. Lawrence.   *Smithsonian Miscellaneous Collections*, vol. 19 (1879), p. 486-88.

This checklist of 128 species of birds that occur in the Lesser Antilles is useful even though those found on Montserrat are not specifically separated out.

98 **Some birds from Montserrat.**
James Bond. *The Auk*, vol. 56 (1939), p. 193-95.
This is a list of bird specimens that the author collected in Montserrat, with brief
discussions of their subspecies status.

Amphibians, reptiles and marine animals

99 **Fishes of the Caribbean reefs.**
Ian F. Took. London: Macmillan Caribbean, 92p.
This illustrated guide to the reef fishes of the Caribbean Sea is useful to snorkellers,
sports fishers and other non-specialists interested in reef species.

100 **Foraging ecology of *Anolis lividus*, an endemic lizard on Montserrat.**
G. R. Brooks. *Virginia Journal of Science*, vol. 32, no. 3 (1981),
p. 87.
This is a report on the food and feeding behaviour of a lizard that is found only on
Montserrat, where it is widely distributed.

101 **Marine life of the Caribbean.**
Alick Jones. London: Macmillan Caribbean, 1978. 90p.
This is an illustrated introduction to the marine life of the Caribbean. It is part of
Macmillan's ongoing series of illustrated handbooks aimed at the non-specialist that
includes *Trees of the Caribbean* (q.v.), *Flowers of the Caribbean* (q.v.) and *Fishes of
the Caribbean reefs* (q.v.).

102 **An observation of *Iguana iguana* feeding.**
W. J. Arendt. *Caribbean Journal of Science*, vol. 22, no. 3-4 (1986),
p. 221-22.
This brief research note describes a young iguana feeding on eggs of the cattle egret at
Fox's Bay, Montserrat.

103 **Seashell treasures of the Caribbean.**
Lesley Sutty. London: Macmillan Caribbean, 1986. 128p.
An illustrated guide to the shells found in the Caribbean aimed at the non-specialist. It is
part of the same introductory natural history series as *Marine life of the Caribbean* (q.v.).

104 **Taxonomic and eco-ethological study of an amphibian of the Lesser
Antilles, *Leptodactylus fallax*.**
J. Lescure. *Bulletin of the Museum of Natural History, Section A:
Zoology, Biology, Ecology*, vol. 1, no. 3 (1979), p. 757-74.
The amphibian *Leptodactylus fallax* Mueller, once more widely spread in the Lesser
Antilles, is now found only on Montserrat and Dominica. This article, based on field
observation, draws attention to the features that distinguish it from similar species, and
describes its colour, vocalization, reproduction, life cycle and diet.

Insects

105 **Butterflies and other insects of the eastern Caribbean.**
Peter D. Stiling. London: Macmillan Caribbean, 1986. 85p.
This is one of Macmillan's series of illustrated handbooks to the plants and animals of
the Caribbean. Like the other volumes in the series published so far (q.v.) it is useful
to the interested non-specialist.

106 **The butterflies of Montserrat.**
Albert Schwartz, Carlos J. Jimenez. *Bulletin of the Allyn Museum*,
University of Florida, no. 66 (March 1982), p. 1-18.
The authors synthesize butterfly systematics for the island of Montserrat, basing their
scheme on both species noted in the literature and on new collection. They describe
thirty-eight species, and compare the incidence of species on Montserrat with St.
Christopher and Guadeloupe.

107 **Collection records of the project 'Mosquitoes of Middle America', part
4, Leeward Islands: Anguilla, Antigua, Barbuda, Montserrat, Nevis, St.
Kitts.**
J. N. Belkin, S. J. Heinemann. *Mosquito Systematics*, vol. 8, no. 2
(1976), p. 123-62.
This collection project aimed to collect and systematize the mosquito species of Central
America and the Caribbean region. Part 4 includes Montserrat among the Leeward
Islands. The collections made in Montserrat are grouped together (as they are for each
island) and the locations where the collections were made are carefully identified.

108 **A field guide to the butterflies of the West Indies.**
N. D. Riley. London: Collins Publications (1975). 258p.
An illustrated and complete field handbook for the identification of butterflies found in
the West Indies, including Montserrat. All species are illustrated and a descriptive
account is given that includes habits, habitat, and scientific and popular names.

109 **Les scorpions des Petites Antilles: approche biogéographique.** (The
scorpions of the Lesser Antilles: biogeographical approach.).
W. R. Lourenco. *Bulletin de la Société Zoologique de France*, vol.
112, no. 3-4, p. 355-62.
Of the two families and thirteen species of scorpions found in the Lesser Antilles, one
species is peculiar to Montserrat, as some other species are also pecular to other
islands. Only two species are widely distributed throughout the Lesser Antilles.

Caribbean Conservation News.
See item no. 316.

Archaeology

General and regional

110 **Caribbean.**
Irving Rouse, Louis Allaire. In: *Chronologies in New World Archaeology*. Edited by R. E. Taylor, Clement W. Meighan. New York: Academic Press, 1978, p. 431-81.

This article summarizes what was known in 1978 about the dates and successions of native American cultures that occupied the eastern half of the Caribbean Basin before and at the time of the European invasion. The article is useful for anyone who wants a regional and chronological context for later work on Montserratian archaeology, such as David Watters's *Transect surveying and prehistoric site locations on Barbuda and Montserrat, Leeward Islands, West Indies* (q.v.).

111 **Early man in the West Indies.**
Jose M. Cruxent, Irving Rouse. *Scientific American*, vol. 221, no. 5 (1969), p. 42-52.

This article summarizes information as of 1969 about the aboriginal settling of the West Indies. The authors depart from the prevailing idea that human beings arrived in the Caribbean region 2,000 years ago, and argue for a date of 7,000 years ago.

112 **Lowland South America and the Antilles.**
Betty J. Meggers, Clifford Evans. In: *Ancient native America*. Edited by Jesse D. Jennings. San Francisco: W. H. Freeman & Co., 1978, p. 543-92.

This article discusses the prehistory of the area from western Cuba south to Tierra del Fuego, and from the Atlantic Ocean to the beginning of the Andes Mountains in the west. Within this large realm, the chronology and archaeology of the Antilles are located in the context of lowland South America. Thus the article is useful in conjunction with the regionally-focused Rouse and Allaire survey, 'Caribbean' (q.v.).

26

Both articles include original synthesis and hypothesis, and bear on the understanding of prehistory in Montserrat.

113 **Pattern and process in West Indian archaeology.**
Irving Rouse. *World Archaeology*, vol. 91, no. 1 (1977), p. 1-11.
This article briefly reviews the course of archaeological research in the West Indies and classifies this research according to the inferences about prehistoric societies it allows us to make. Archaeological study ranges from the simple collection and classification of material remains on the first level, to inferences about people who produced those remains on the second, to inferences about sociocultural systems and ecological relationships on the third, and to generalizations about the principles of social and cultural change on the fourth. West Indian archaeological interpretation has only recently begun to enter the third and fourth levels.

114 **Prehistory of the West Indies.**
Irving Rouse. *Science*, vol. 144, no. 3618 (1964), p. 499-513.
The West Indian islands are especially interesting to students of the indigenous cultures of the Americas because they link three mainland regions – Yucatán, Florida and northeastern South America – and thus suggest a range of questions concerning the peopling of the islands. This article describes the natural setting, the basic and shared features of indigenous culture, the dating and succession of cultures and a synthesis of research to 1965. Although it was written before research into Montserrat's prehistory had yet begun, it provides a useful introduction to the Amerindians of the Lesser Antilles and a framework into which later archaeological research on Montserrat can be fitted.

Montserrat's prehistory

115 **A problematic artifact from Trants, Montserrat.**
David R. Watters. *Journal of the Virgin Islands Archaeological Society*, no. 9 (1980), p. 18-21.
The author describes an unidentified stone object that was pulled from its prehistoric context without proper archaeological procedure, and hence can be neither dated nor associated with a known tradition. So far the object appears to be unique among aboriginal materials from the West Indies.

116 **Thin section petrography of northern Lesser Antilles ceramics.**
Jack Donahue, David R. Watters, Sarah Millspaugh.
Geoarchaeology, vol. 5, no. 3 (1990), p. 229-54.
Using a petrographic microscope, the authors examined thin sections from forty-four potsherds taken from eight prehistoric sites distributed on the islands of Montserrat, Barbuda, Anguilla and St. Martin. Petrographic analysis of the pottery showed grains of volcanic and carbonate rock, and fragments of pre-existing pottery, called 'grog'. The Montserrat prehistoric sherds show a predominance of volcanic grains used as temper, along with some beach sand. Later historic, slave-made ceramics indicate the

same method of earthenware manufacture, and thus point to continuity from prehistoric times.

117 **Transect surveying and prehistoric site locations on Barbuda and Montserrat, Leeward Islands, West Indies.**
David Robert Watters. PhD thesis, University of Pittsburgh, 1980. 421p. (Available from University Microfilms Ann Arbor, Michigan, order no. 8112643).

This thesis, based on archaeological field research in Montserrat and Barbuda, investigates the relationship between physical and biotic environmental factors and the location of prehistoric living sites. The two islands present contrasting environments: Montserrat is mountainous, volcanic, well-watered and densely vegetated in most areas; Barbuda is a flat, dry, coral island. Survey data indicate that people of the Saladoid culture occupied Montserrat about 1,800 years ago. They favoured locations close to the coast, near streams, with good planting soil and easy access to the ocean. The thesis also includes some information on the archaeology of Montserrat's historic sites.

118 **Utility of a transect survey technique in Caribbean prehistoric studies: applications on Barbuda and Montserrat.**
David R. Watters, Richard Scaglion. *Proceedings of the Eighth International Congress for the Study of the Pre-Columbian Cultures of the Lesser Antilles*, Anthropological Research Paper no. 22 (1980), p. 338-47.

A report on an archaeological sampling technique applied to two physically and ecologically dissimilar islands of the Lesser Antilles, Montserrat and Barbuda, and its limitations. The authors suggest improvements and modifications that might make this transect survey technique useful in disclosing prehistoric settlement patterns in the Lesser Antilles.

119 **Vertebrates from archaeological sites on Montserrat, West Indies.**
David W. Steadman, David R. Watters, Elizabeth J. Reitz, Gregory K. Pregill. *Annals of Carnegie Museum*, vol. 53 (1984), p. 1-29.

Analysis of vertebrate remains from two archaeological sites on Montserrat, representing the Saladoid culture of about 2,000 years ago, yielded information about human diet and prehistoric human-animal relationships on the island. Fish and sea turtle remains show that the Saladoid people used marine resources; land vertebrates included iguana, doves, rodents, agouti and dog. The two last mammals are not indigenous to the island, and were apparently brought there by the Saladoid people.

Historical archaeology

120 **Afro-Montserratian ceramics from the Harney Site cemetery, Montserrat, West Indies.**
James B. Petersen, David R. Watters. *Annals of Carnegie Museum*, vol. 57 (1988), p. 167-87.

The skeletons of seventeen black slaves were recovered from an unmarked eighteenth-century burial ground in Montserrat, along with twenty sherds representing approximately eight ceramic pots. Analysis of the potsherds places them within the tradition of similar sherds found elsewhere in the West Indies, a tradition that is derived from African techniques of coil-building ceramic vessels fired in an open hearth. The sherds date from the late eighteenth century and their presence in the graves is most likely adventitious rather than deliberate.

121 **Archaeology on the Galways plantation.**
Conrad M. Goodwin. *Florida Anthropologist*, vol. 34, no. 4 (December 1982), p. 251-57.

This article reports on the excavation of a sugar-boiling house at Galways, an eighteenth-century sugar plantation in Montserrat. Research on the sugar-boiling house is part of a larger interdisciplinary project on the history and historical archaeology of Galways.

122 **Description of skeletal remains from a black slave cemetery from Montserrat, West Indies.**
Robert W. Mann, Lee Meadows, William M. Bass, David R. Watters. *Annals of Carnegie Museum*, vol. 56 (1987), p. 319-36.

Skeletal remains of West Indian slaves are not plentiful, so the seventeen individuals buried at the Harney Site cemetery in Montserrat, dating from the eighteenth century and identified as black, represent an important find that supplies information on health and disease, nutrition, stature and age at death. These skeletal remains are marked by anaemia, fractures, malnutrition, osteoarthritis, and possibly a case of leprosy – all evidence of harsh conditions during life.

123 **An 18th century plantation support structure on the Caribbean Island of Montserrat.**
Sarah Zacks. Unpublished Master's thesis, Brown University, Providence, Rhode Island, 1985. 56p.

A report on the excavation of an eighteenth-century building of undetermined use on the Galways plantation site. The thesis reviews hypotheses about its use, and includes drawings, based on archaeological evidence, of what the building might have looked like had it been used for cooperage, carpentry, stabling or storage. The thesis also includes analyses of ceramic remains and pipestems. Photocopies are available from the Department of Anthropology, Brown University, Providence, Rhode Island, USA 02912 at a cost of US$10.00.

124 **Excavations at the Harney Site slave cemetery, Montserrat, West Indies.**
David R. Watters. *Annals of Carnegie Museum*, vol. 56 (1987),
p. 289-318.

This report on the excavation of a slave burial ground that was accidentally uncovered during house construction focuses on the patterns of burial and on the artifacts recovered on the site. All graves were dug down to an underlying rock stratum; the bodies were oriented east-west, with heads toward the west; bodies were laid fully extended on their backs; and the presence of nails suggests the use of coffins. The artifacts show that this cemetery, hitherto unknown and unrecorded, was in use until at least the end of the eighteenth century.

125 **Galways plantation project.**
Lydia Mihelic Pulsipher. *Caribbean Geography*, vol. 1, no. 2 (1983),
p. 141-42.

Reports the beginning of an interdisciplinary study of the eighteenth-century sugar estate in Montserrat, Galways plantation. The study aims to synthesize archaeological, historical, and geographical research.

126 **A sugar-boiling house at Galways: an Irish sugar plantation in Montserrat, West Indies.**
Lydia Mihelic Pulsipher, Conrad M. Goodwin. *Post-Medieval Archaeology*, vol. 16 (1982), p. 21-27.

This report describes the eighteenth-century sugar-boiling house at Galways plantation, in St. Patrick's parish of Montserrat. The extant ruin was excavated in 1981 as part of a larger project to study Galways plantation and its buildings. The article conveys useful information about the construction, equipment and arrangement of a processing structure vital to the dominant sugar and slave economy of the Leeward Islands of the period.

127 **A Turlington Balsam phial from Montserrat, West Indies: genuine or counterfeit?**
David R. Watters. *Historical Archaeology*, vol. 15, no. 1 (1981),
p. 105-08.

The author uncovered a pharmaceutical bottle during the course of excavating an eighteenth-century burial ground, compares it with a very similar Turlington Balsam of Life bottle found at Williamsburg, Virginia, and considers whether the Montserrat specimen is authentic Turlington or one of the numerous eighteenth-century counterfeits. The cello-shaped bottle is dated 1751.

History

General and regional

128 The African exchange: toward a biological history of black people.
Edited by Kenneth F. Kiple.   Durham, North Carolina: Duke
University Press, 1987. 280p. bibliog.
Each essay in this volume is an innovative and well-researched contribution to the
growing understanding of morbidity and mortality among black populations in the
Americas. Among the many important topics covered are the health status of West
Indian recruits into the British army from 1817 to 1914; the history and ecology of
hypertension among living black populations in the Americas; and the relation of
hunger to the Christmas revels of slaves in the British West Indies.

**129 Calendar of State papers, Colonial Series, America and the West Indies,
1574-1737.**
Edited by Noel W. Sainsbury, J. W. Fortescue.   London: HMSO,
1860-1903. 43 vols.
These volumes briefly describe the contents of selected documents relating to the
British colonies in the Americas that are held at the Public Record Office, London.
The descriptions are arranged chronologically, dated, numbered consecutively and
indexed by place. Thus one may find all the references to Montserrat in the index. The
calendar contains much useful documentary information and may be used by itself as a
source; it is also used as a key to the original documents.

130 Caribbeana.
Vere Oliver.   London: Mitchell, Hughes, & Clark, 1912-1914. 4 vols.
A printed compilation transcribed from selected manuscript sources relating to the
British Caribbean from the seventeenth to the nineteenth centuries. The documents
were chosen for their potential usefulness to genealogists, but other valuable historical
information can be gleaned from them. Montserrat items, for example, include the

census of 1677-1678 (q.v.), a list of early nineteenth-century wills (vol. 3, p. 119), accounts of debts from 1653-55 transcribed from the Egerton Mss. (vol. 2, p. 222-24), and eighteenth- and nineteenth-century records of the Dyett family (vol.4, p. 145-54).

131 History of Alliouagana.
Howard A. Fergus. Plymouth, Montserrat: University Centre, 1975. 72p. bibliog.

This book is made up of eleven chapters that deal with the European discovery of Montserrat, the orginal Amerindian inhabitants, the period of slave-worked sugar plantations, and more recent religion, politics, labour, education and contemporary affairs on the island. It also includes a chronology of important dates and a short bibliography.

132 History of Alliouagana: a short history of Montserrat.
Howard A. Fergus. Plymouth, Montserrat: Montserrat Printery, 1985. 64p.

A different version – not merely a new edition – of the author's 1975 booklet of the same title (q.v.), this is a short review of Montserratian history based on secondary sources and on a few documents available in print. *Alliouagana* is said to be a Carib word meaning 'island of the aloe plant'. Fergus is a Montserratian historian, political figure and resident tutor at the extra-mural division of the University of the West Indies that is located on Montserrat.

133 History of the British West Indies.
Sir Alan Burns. London: George Allen & Unwin, 1965. 849p. bibliog.

This is a general history and description of those Caribbean territories that were or are British colonies, written from a colonial point of view. It covers aboriginal inhabitants, early exploration and settlement by Europeans, and subsequent periods in chronological order into the twentieth century. The chapter devoted to each period is further subdivided by topics and territories. The index is excellent, and is an essential tool for following the history of any particular place, such as Montserrat.

134 Ireland's only colony: records of Montserrat.
T. Savage English. Typescript, 1930.

Montserrat's historical documents have not survived well in their storage place in the Montserrat Courthouse, and since the nearly total destruction of the island by hurricane Hugo in 1989 are in all likelihood gone. Many are duplicated in the Public Record Office, London. English was a British colonial administrator who used the extant manuscripts in Montserrat to compile a brief history of the island that includes material on seventeenth-century settlement, slavery and sugar plantations, emancipation and recent Montserrat. Unfortunately he did not list the documents he used or cite his sources. One copy was on file in the Montserrat Public Library; a second copy is available at the Institute of Commonwealth Studies of the University of London.

135 **A short history of the West Indies.**
J. H. Parry, Philip Sherlock. London: Macmillan, 1971. 3rd ed. 337p.
bibliog.
This history of the Caribbean islands begins with the Columbian invasion. It is regional
in scope, but the formerly British Caribbean receives emphasis. It is notable because
the original edition (1956) was the first history of the region that was written from a
Caribbean point of view and that treats the region as a geographical unit in itself, and
not merely as a diverse cluster of economic or political appendages to European
metropoles. It is an excellent introductory history with a useful list of suggested further
readings.

Early colonial period to 1710

136 **The accounts of a colonial governor's agent in the seventeenth century.**
C. S. S. Higham. *American Historical Review*, vol. 28 (1923), p. 263-
85.
A published transcription of the personal accounts of William Stapleton, second
governor of the Leeward Islands and lieutenant governor of Montserrat in the 1670s.
These accounts have not yet been studied, and are a valuable source for insights into
the expenses, material possessions, spending priorities, values and style of life of a
colonial official and landowner. They are not to be confused with Stapleton's surviving
public accounts of Montserrat, noted in Higham's *Some treasurer's accounts of
Montserrat* (q.v.) and studied in detail in Berleant-Schiller's *Free labor and the
economy in seventeenth-century Montserrat* (q.v.).

137 **The British empire in America.**
John Oldmixon. London, 1708. 2 vols.
It is wise to bring some scepticism to the reading of Oldmixon. His work is
idiosyncratic and retells hearsay, but it is one of the few sources we have for the late
seventeenth century that ranges widely over the British Caribbean. It also has some
value in showing how the Caribbean colonies were popularly perceived in England.
Montserrat is covered in the second volume.

138 **Cromwell's policy of transportation, Parts I and II.**
Aubrey Gwynn, S. J., M. A. *Studies: An Irish Quarterly of Letters*,
1930 (December), p. 607-23, and 1931 (June), p. 291-305.
Cromwell's Puritan government adopted a policy of sending Irish priests, political
prisoners and prisoners of war to the English colonies of the West Indies, where they
were usually sold as indentured servants. Gwynn has gleaned the manuscript sources
relating to this policy, documenting the transportation and describing specific incidents
and persons. Much of the seventeenth-century population of Montserrat was made up
of transported Irish indentured servants.

139 **The development of the Leeward Islands under the Restoration, 1660-1688.**
C. S. S. Higham. Cambridge, England: Cambridge University Press, 1921. 226p. bibliog.

This is a study of the growth of colonial government, the plantation economy and the slave trade in England's developing Leeward Islands Colony, of which Montserrat was part. It also deals with the control of the colony by the Lords of Trade and Plantations.

140 **Early Irish emigration to the West Indies. Parts I and II.**
Aubrey Gwynn, S. J., M. A. *Studies: An Irish Quarterly of Letters*, 1929 (June), p. 377-93, and 1929 (December), p. 648-63.

Gwynn's compilation of references to the Irish immigrants of the West Indies in the seventeenth century includes many from colonial documents and literature of the period. Part I deals with the early seventeenth-century Irish presence in the entire region from Virginia to the Amazon; Part II deals specifically with Montserrat and St. Christopher's, where Irish settlers, indentured servants and freed men and women who had completed their bondservice were a numerically, though not politically, dominant element in the population.

141 **Free labor and the economy in seventeenth-century Montserrat.**
Riva Berleant-Schiller. *The William and Mary Quarterly*, 3rd series, vol. 46, no. 3, p. 539-64.

The author uses the public account books kept by Governor William Stapleton between 1672 and 1680, the Montserrat census of 1667-78 (q.v.) and documents stored in the Public Record Office, London, to reconstruct aspects of the domestic economy of Montserrat and the lives of free white wage workers. She shows that low wages, high prices, colonial policies that favoured slavery and sugar estates, legislative constraints, restricted access to land and competition from a rising slave work force all created harsh conditions that effectively checked the growth of a free white labour force.

142 **The historical notes of the early years of the island of Montserrat.**
George I. Mendes. *Leeward Islands Review and Caribbean Digest*, vol. 1, no. 7 (1937), p. 9-17.

This is a brief sketch of the settlement of Montserrat from 1623 to 1632, with digressions on Montserrat's agricultural potential, on the disintegration of Montserrat's documents and on the early settlement of St. Kitts and Antigua. It is interesting as a local attempt to unearth and preserve documentary evidence of early settlement, but the article lacks any references to the documents consulted.

143 **Mounseratt, 1677-8.**
Edited by Vere Langford Oliver. *Caribbeana* (q.v.), vol. 2. (1912), p. 316-20, 342-47.

A transcription from Colonial Office records in the Public Record Office, London, of the census that William Stapleton, second governor of the Leeward Islands Colony, ordered to be taken in 1677-78. It includes the names of most of the white men and a few white women on the island and the division or district in which they resided.

Children, slaves, most women and some white male indentured servants are left unnamed, although they are enumerated by division.

144 **No peace beyond the line: the English in the Caribbean, 1624-1690.**
Carl Bridenbaugh, Roberta Bridenbaugh. New York: Oxford University Press, 1972. 440p. maps. bibliog.

Written from 'the insular rather than the imperial point of view', this volume argues that the seventeenth-century English colonies in the Caribbean, including Montserrat, were not merely social failures, but also human tragedies. The English colonies failed to become stable, working societies on the model of the mother country because the settlers were motivated by greed rather than by conscious efforts to create and sustain English institutions. The failure was turned to tragedy by slavery and the high death rates of Africans forcibly imported. Only the slaves were able to create any kind of community life for themselves, but the enormity of the English failure crippled any other healthy social development in the colonies.

145 **Some treasurer's accounts of Montserrat, 1672-81.**
C. S. S. Higham. *English Historical Review*, vol. 38 (1923), p. 87-90.

This short comment simply notes the existence of the public accounts of Montserrat and interprets them as evidence of the attempts of the Lords of Trade and Plantation (precursor of the Colonial Office) to keep track of colonial finances. The accounts are part of the Stapleton Mss., a collection of papers relating to the Stapleton family that begins with William Stapleton, lieutenant governor of Montserrat and second governor of the Leeward Islands in the 1670s, and continues into the eighteenth century. Riva Berleant-Schiller examined these public accounts in detail in her study *Free labor and the economy in seventeenth-century Montserrat* (q.v.); J. R. V. Johnston used the wills, deeds and letters in the collection for his study *The Stapleton sugar plantations in the Leeward Islands* (q.v.).

146 **Sugar and slaves: the rise of the planter class in the English West Indies, 1624-1713.**
Richard S. Dunn. Chapel Hill, North Carolina: University of North Carolina Press, 1972. 359p. maps. bibliog.

Dunn concludes, as do Bridenbaugh and Bridenbaugh in *No peace beyond the line* (q.v.), that the seventeenth-century English colonies in the Caribbean were social failures, but his analysis is much more sophisticated. Dunn recognizes that the social disaster in the English Caribbean was not the failure to reproduce English institutions, but rather the nature of the dominant institutions that did develop – the plantation economy based on sugar production, and the class system characterized by a small and powerful élite and a large slave labour force. These institutions answered the English colonists' single goal of maximum material gain; other goals were unimportant to them. This volume includes information specifically related to Montserrat, and helps the reader understand Montserrat as a seventeenth-century Caribbean sugar colony.

147 **White servitude in colonial America: an economic analysis.**
David W. Galenson.   Cambridge, England: Cambridge University
Press, 1981. 291p. bibliog.
Written by an economic historian, this is the standard contemporary work on
indentured servitude. It is important for Montserrat because it illuminates the question
of Irish immigration in the seventeenth century and contributes to an understanding of
the transformation of the plantation force from European indentured servants to
African slaves.

Plantations, slavery and emancipation (1710-1834)

148 **Absentee landlordism in the British Caribbean, 1750-1833.**
Lowell Joseph Ragatz.   *Agricultural History*, vol. 5, no. 1 (1931), p. 7-
24.
This article describes the damaging effects on the West Indian colonies of absentee
landlords who lived in England, leaving the supervision of their estates to attorneys.
Ragatz particularly discusses Montserrat as a place where effective government could
not be carried on because there were not enough eligible people (that is to say, free
white property owners) to fill the necessary offices competently.

149 **The development of the British West Indies, 1700-1763.**
Frank Wesley Pitman.   New Haven, Connecticut: Yale University
Press, 1917. Reprinted, Hamden, Connecticut: Archon Books, 1970.
495p.
This seminal work is essential to an understanding of the West Indian sugar islands,
their society and economy, and their role in British imperial history. Pitman showed
the development of societies based on the investment of large amounts of capital,
plantation production that was industrial in its organization, and abundant slave
labour. Pitman argued that slavery was an uneconomic form of labour, that politically
successful sugar interests achieved a monopoly despite the outrageous costs of
producing sugar, and that planter domination of the economy of British America
opened the way for the American Revolution. The book includes specific information
on Montserrat, but is especially valuable to the student of Montserrat history because
of its general and contextual treatment of West Indian society, slavery, political
influence and plantation economies in the eighteenth century.

150 **The diary of John Baker.**
Edited by Philip C. Yorke.   London: Hutchinson & Co., 1931.
John Baker was Solicitor General of the Leeward Islands, and resided there from 1751
to 1759. This volume consists of extracts from the diary he kept. His wife, Mary Ryan,
came from Montserrat, and the diary contains many references to persons of
Montserrat, with comments about their behaviour, their slaves and the behaviour of
slaves. It yields many interesting insights into planter social life and relationships.

151 **The history of sugar.**
Noel Deerr. London: Cassell, 1941. 2 vols.
This world history of sugar has not yet been superseded, and since Montserrat was a sugar island in the eighteenth century, a great deal of information on Montserrat's sugar economy can be found in the work, including annual production and export figures.

152 **Report for the year 1829.**
Incorporated Society for the Conversion and Religious Instruction and Education of the Negro Slaves in the British West India Islands.
London: William Clowes, 1829.
The section on Montserrat reports on the lack of money for slave education and the indifference of the planter class to the problem, even though slave education had been mandated by British amelioration legislation in the 1820s. Nevertheless, some slaves attended Sunday schools taught and financed by Nonconformist missionary societies.

153 **Resource management strategies on an eighteenth century Caribbean sugar plantation.**
Lydia Mihelic Pulsipher. *Florida Anthropologist*, vol. 35, no. 4 (December 1982), p. 243-50.
The author explains her hypotheses about the siting and the water management techniques of Galways plantation in the eighteenth century. The article is based on long-term historical and archaeological research on Galways.

154 **Slave populations of the British Caribbean, 1807-1834.**
Barry W. Higman. Baltimore, Maryland: Johns Hopkins University Press, 1984. 781p. maps. bibliog.
In this definitive and comprehensive work Higman synthesizes the available information on the slave populations in the British Caribbean colonies from the abolition of international slave trading in 1807 to emancipation in 1834. Information on Montserrat's slave population includes data on fertility, natural increase, manumissions, intercolonial trade after 1807, provision grounds, and population size and density.

155 **Slave society in the British Leeward Islands at the end of the eighteenth century.**
Elsa V. Goveia. New Haven, Connecticut: Yale University Press, 1965. 370p. map. bibliog.
The Leeward Islands Colony in the eighteenth century consisted of Antigua, St. Christopher (now called St. Kitts), Nevis, Montserrat, Anguilla, Barbuda and the British Virgin Islands. Goveia discusses these as a group that, taken together, yields a more representative synthesis of slave and plantation society than could a single island. These colonies developed and matured as economies founded mainly on plantation production and institutionalized slavery. The end of the eighteenth century was the period during which these 'mature' slave societies began to undergo the stresses of economic, political and ideological change emanating from Great Britain. Goveia's work, based on documents in the Public Record Office, London, is a classic that has not been superseded. It covers the political system, the slave and sugar system and the

class organization of Leeward islands society, and includes a discussion of the slave laws and of the effects of Christian missionization.

156 The Stapleton sugar plantations in the Leeward Islands.
J. R. V. Johnston. *Bulletin of the John Rylands Library*, vol. 48 (1965), p. 175-206.

The author based his study of the Stapleton family plantations, including their holdings on Montserrat, on the deeds, wills and letters included in the Stapleton Mss. of the Rylands Library at the University of Manchester. William Staplcton was sccond governor of the Leeward Islands and Lieutenant Governor of Montserrat in the 1670s.

157 Sugar and slavery.
Richard B. Sheridan. Baltimore, Maryland: Johns Hopkins University Press, 1974. 314p. bibliog.

This history of sugar production and slavery in the West Indies covers the period from the mid-seventeenth century to the end of the eighteenth century. Chapter eight deals specifically with the Leeward Islands (p. 148-69) and with Montserrat (p. 170-83). It supplies valuable information, based on a manuscript 1729 census, on population, size and ownership of plantations, plantation livestock and equipment, and other economic and demographic data for the first third of the eighteenth century. It also includes interesting and unusual material on the careers and activities of large and small planters.

158 The West Indies and the development of colonial government, 1801-1834.
D. J. Murray. Oxford, England: Clarendon Press, 1965. 264p. bibliog.

This is an important work on the British governing of its West India colonies during the period of the abolition of the slave trade (1807) and the final emancipation of slaves in 1834. During this time the British Colonial Office developed into an independent bureaucracy with clearly defined responsibilities and principles of operation, a process that began in 1801 when colonial administration was moved from the Home Department to the Secretary of State for War. Murray briefly reviews the governmental relations between Britain and the colonies in the eighteenth century, explores the changing relationship of the British government and colonial governments after 1801, explains the internal self-governing of legislative colonies, shows how the Colonial Office took shape, and explains its functioning during and after the emancipation process. Montserrat is specifically mentioned, but the value of this book for the student of Montserrat's history is more general and contextual, as it clarifies the nature of colonial governments and their relationship to the Colonial Office during a critical period of West Indian history.

Post-emancipation

159 Five of the Leewards, 1834-1870.
Douglas Hall. Barbados: Caribbean Universities Press, 1971. 211p. bibliog.

This volume focuses on the problems that five islands – Antigua, Barbuda, Montserrat, Nevis and St. Kitts (by the nineteenth century no longer called St. Christopher) – faced during the period following slave emancipation in 1834. Among the chief problems in Montserrat were resistance to plantation labour on the part of the freed slaves, the need to diversify agricultural production, the thwarting of land ownership and peasant production for the freed population, and general poverty and demoralization.

160 The growth of the modern West Indies.
Gordon K. Lewis. London: MacGibbon & Kee, 1968. 506p. map. bibliog.

This book deals with the English-speaking islands of the Caribbean from about 1918 to 1966, which the author calls 'the modern formative period'. It is not merely a history of events; it is an historical consideration of the making of West Indian society in the twentieth century by a scholar who has long resided in the Caribbean and taught at the Institute of Caribbean Studies at the University of Puerto Rico.

161 The island of Montserrat: its history and development.
G. R. Alexander. Carlisle, England: Hudson Scott & Sons, 1886. 24p.

A very brief sketch of Montserrat's history from 1632 to the late nineteenth century in what is essentially an advertising tract for lime juice. A long decline in the sugar economy began around 1802. One of the schemes planned to mitigate that decline was the cultivation of lime trees, which was begun in 1852. By 1886 Montserrat was the largest producer of lime juice for the English market. (Dominica later superseded Montserrat as a lime juice exporter.)

162 The West Indies, before and since slave emancipation.
John Davy. London: W. and F. G. Cash, 1854. 424p.

This report is based on material collected during three years' residence in the West Indies. Chapter 13 deals with Montserrat, where natural disasters and epidemics exacerbated societal deterioration following emancipation. It provides useful information on population, emigration, the hardships of former slaves, and economic decline owing to neglect and mismanagement of labour.

Seventeenth century Montserrat: an environmental impact statement.
See item no. 19.

The West Indies: patterns of development, culture and environmental change since 1492.
See item no. 20.

Six months in the West Indies in 1825.
See item no. 35.

The West Indies in 1837.
See item no. 36.

Commissioners' report on justice.
See item no. 210.

The early laws of Montserrat (1668-1680).
See item no. 211.

Documents relating to the Irish in the West Indies.
See item no. 279.

A guide for the study of British Caribbean history, 1763-1834.
See item no. 337.

Historical dictionary of the British Caribbean.
See item no. 338.

Population

163 **The aging of the population of Montserrat: causes and consequences.**
G. Edward Ebanks. *Population Index*, vol. 54, no. 3 (1988), p. 452.
Even though Montserrat is a developing country, its demographic profile differs from
the usual pattern of developing countries in that the population is aging. Median and
mean age are high and fertility, already low, is declining. Immigrant retirees, returning
migrants and the emigration of the young all contribute to the aging of the population.
The statistically low level of unemployment is due to the number of residents over
sixty-five, and the rising crude death rate is a result of the aging of the population.

164 **Demographic survey of the British colonial empire: vol. III, West Indian
and American territories.**
R. R. Kuczynski. London: Oxford University Press, 1953. 497p.
bibliog.
The author has systematically surveyed and abstracted all available census information
from the former British colonies. The Montserrat section (p. 311-21) covers the years
1891 to 1946, and includes tables on total population; composition of population by
age, sex, birthplace and marital status; and birth, death and marriage registration.
There are also tables that compare the years 1921 and 1946.

165 **Montserrat population projection, 2000.**
Consumer Markets Abroad, (March 1988), p. 2.
This brief article estimates the growth of Montserrat's population to the year 2000.
Births are predicted to continue to exceed deaths and the number of children under
sixteen will grow. The total population, however, will not expand appreciably because
of continued adult emigration.

166 **The population of the British colonies in America before 1776.**
Robert V. Wells. Princeton, New Jersey: Princeton University Press,
1975. 342p. bibliog.
This comprehensive work of historical demography covers all the British colonies of
the Americas before the War of Independence. It provides many valuable details about

Population

population in Montserrat and the Leeward Islands in comparative framework from 1678 to 1776, including age and sex structure, condition of servitude, skin colour, ethnic ascription, and the composition and organization of households (p. 209-31; p. 269-333).

Society and Social Conditions

General and regional

167 **The Caribbean region.**
Sidney W. Mintz.   In: *Slavery, colonialism, and racism.* Edited by
Sidney W. Mintz. New York: Norton, 1974, p. 45-71.
It is difficult to make significant general statements about the Caribbean, consisting as
it does of so many small and scattered land areas, each with its own particular features.
Nevertheless, Mintz's attempt is successful and illuminating. Some common themes of
Afro-Caribbean experience that he points out are a long history of colonial
exploitation and slavery, economic scarcity, absences or perceived absences of
economic opportunity, ethnic heterogeneity and stratification based on colour. All of
these apply to Montserrat.

168 **Caribbean transformations.**
Sidney W. Mintz.   Chicago: Aldine, 1974. 355p.
This book, along with David Lowenthal's *West Indian societies* (q.v.), is required
reading for understanding the Caribbean region or any of its parts. Mintz focuses on
Afro-Caribbean culture and society. He discusses African antecedents, the experience
of slavery and the plantation, and the rise and nature of Afro-Caribbean peasantries as
a distinctive adaptation in the region.

169 **Family land and Caribbean society: toward an ethnography of Afro-
Caribbean peasantries.**
Jean Besson.   In: *Perspectives on Caribbean regional identity.* Edited
by Elizabeth Thomas-Hope. Liverpool, England: Centre for Latin
American Studies, University of Liverpool, 1984, p. 57-83.
'Family land' is a kind of rural land tenure widespread in the Caribbean. In this folk
tenure system the land is not divisible, and is bequeathed jointly to all children of the
owners who are born in wedlock. Thus the joint owners may use the land, but do not

own bits of it individually. Besson argues that this form of tenure is a creative Afro-Caribbean adaptation that took shape in the Caribbean and is important in sustaining Afro-Caribbean peasant values and identity. In Montserrat, family land is a prestigious form of land tenure in rural villages, and as many as five generations may be observed living on it, even if family members carry on subsistence cultivation elsewhere.

170 **Montserrat – autonomy in microcosm.**
David Lowenthal. Mimeographed typescript, 1961. 110p.

A report on the human geography, social organization and social structure of Montserrat based on field research undertaken by a geographer in the late 1950s. A copy is on file at the American Geographical Society collection, held at the library of the University of Wisconsin at Milwaukee, Wisconsin, USA.

171 **A typology of rural community forms in the Caribbean.**
Michael M. Horowitz. *Anthropological Quarterly*, vol. 33 (1960), p. 177-87.

Horowitz proposes that the types of rural community organization in the Caribbean are founded on productive economy and productive technology. He finds a continuum of community types ranging from tightly integrated villages founded on household control over a piece of productive land to loose aggregates associated with plantation wage labour. Most of Montserrat's rural villages fall into Horowitz's category of tightly integrated communities in which a majority of households are at least partly supported by subsistence and small cash agricultural production on small holdings that they own or rent.

172 **West Indian societies.**
David Lowenthal. London: Oxford University Press, 1972. 385p. map. bibliog.

Despite its date of publication, this remains an important synthesizing work on the Caribbean islands that manages to derive significant generalizations about society and culture in the region despite the great diversity and range of its small insular societies. The author discusses social structure, race and ethnicity, creolization, migration, national identity and colonialism. The book includes specific references to Montserrat, but it is equally useful for supplying a regional context into which Montserrat may be fitted.

Class and colour

173 **Emigration and the locus of political and economic power: a study in social stratification.**
Allen S. Ehrlich. Mimeographed typescript, 1963. 55p.

Based on anthropological field research in Plymouth, Montserrat's town, this report analyses the relationships among the political, economic and class systems of Montserrat. The author interprets Montserratian stratification as a three-class system based on occupational criteria and modified by factors of skin colour, education and income, and concludes with a discussion of stratification in multi-ethnic societies. This essay can be found at the Research Institute for the Study of Man, 162 East 78th St., New York City 10021, USA.

174 **Montserrat: paradise or prison?**
Howard A. Fergus. *Bulletin of Eastern Caribbean Affairs*, vol. 12, no. 1 (March/April 1986), p. 1-12.
The title of this paper is intended to evoke the polarities in contemporary Montserratian society. The article analyses a policy that encourages Montserrat to be perceived as a paradise by expatriate foreign residents, while at the same time it is a social, economic and political prison for its indigenous inhabitants. Fergus is bitterly and justifiably critical of both foreign and Montserratian attitudes and policies that allow North American resident tourism to shape a bifurcated society with deep and visible differences in wealth, housing, skin colour and nationality. The problem is exacerbated because foreign residents and many Montserratians do not even perceive it.

175 **Race and stratification in the Caribbean.**
M. G. Smith. In: *Corporations and society*. Chicago: Aldine, 1974, p. 271-346.
Smith defines 'stratification' as the unequal distribution of resources, rewards and opportunities among members of a society, and explores the relationship between stratification and race in the Caribbean. He concludes that those who share a given racial ancestry in the Caribbean have become collectivities within society, and that the relative place of these collectivities in the stratification system is generated by political conditions. Fergus's essay, 'Montserrat: paradise or prison?' (q.v.), illustrates this state of affairs in Montserrat.

Gender

176 **Female status and male dominance in Montserrat, West Indies.**
Yolanda T. Moses. PhD thesis, University of California, Riverside, 1976. 243p. (Available from University Microfilms, Ann Arbor, Michigan, USA).
A study of women's status and changing women's roles that considers factors of cultural ideals, women's economic contribution to the household, education, paid employment, marital status, kinship networks and class within the overwhelmingly Afro-Caribbean population of Montserrat. It is based on extended residence and field research that included interviews with women and that emphasizes values, attitudes and women's perceptions of themselves as well as the influence of class. Moses discovered a widespread ideology of male dominance among the women she studied.

177 **Female status, the family, and male dominance in a West Indian community.**
Yolanda T. Moses. *Signs: Journal of Women in Culture and Society*, vol. 3, no. 1 (1977), p. 142-53.

Based on the author's doctoral thesis, this article supports the hypothesis that improved status for women does not necessarily follow from amplified economic contributions to the household, especially if the ideals of a culture grant greater prestige to men's activities. The author measures status by the power to make decisions that affect the household; she is not concerned with status in the wider society. Her research shows that women's status in the household is related to the presence or absence of a husband-father and to the degree that women themselves have internalized the cultural ideologies of male dominance. It is not related to women's contributions in either money or labour.

178 **Gender roles in Caribbean agricultural labour.**
Janet Henshall Momsen. In: *Labour in the Caribbean.* Edited by Malcolm Cross, Gad Heuman. London: Macmillan Caribbean, 1988, p. 141-58.

The author's research in Montserrat contributes to this article on women's roles in agriculture both before and since emancipation. The author argues that since Caribbean peasant agriculture is so heavily dependent on women's labour, a reduction in the conflict between women's agricultural and domestic roles is necessary if peasant cultivation is to become more efficient.

179 **Networks and mobility: the case of West Indian domestics from Montserrat.**
Jane Sawyer Turrittin. *Canadian Review of Sociology and Anthropology*, vol. 13, no. 3 (1976), p. 305-20.

The migration of West Indian women to Canada is directly related to the availability of domestic work. This article describes the experiences of fifteen Montserratian women who had begun their work in Toronto as domestics. It shows how they created and used networks of friendship that eventually helped them to move into white- and blue-collar jobs, advance their educations and achieve lives of expanded independence and autonomy.

180 **Sex differences in a Negro peasant community; Montserrat, B.W.I.**
Theodora M. Abel, Rhoda Métraux. *Journal of Projective Techniques*, vol. 23 (1959), p. 127-33.

This study is based on collaboration between a psychologist (Abel) and an anthropologist (Métraux). They administered a series of projective tests to a sample of the population of a rural village, and analysed the results for sex differences in personality and psychological characteristics. Some small attempt is made to relate the characteristics that the tests reportedly show to the economic and social milieu, and to compare, however briefly, the results to other cross-cultural studies based on projective testing.

181 **What price education: the working women of Montserrat.**
Yolanda T. Moses. *Anthropology and Education Quarterly*, vol. 6,
no. 3 (1975), p. 13-16.
The author considers the effects of paid outside employment on the role of working
women as household decision-makers. Her research shows that cultural traditions of
male dominance among middle-class married and single women outweigh factors of
education and occupation. Working-class women, however, exercised more autonomy
regardless of education, occupation or marital status.

The individual in society

182 **Differential responses to projective testing in a Negro peasant
community: Montserrat, B.W.I.**
Theodora M. Abel. *International Journal of Social Psychiatry*, vol. 6
(1960), p. 218-24.
This paper discusses some of the more individualistic responses to a series of projective
tests administered to a sample of the population in a rural village in Montserrat in 1953
and 1954, and attempts to interpret individual psychodynamics from them.

183 **The dispersion of significance in a changing culture: Montserrat,
B.W.I.**
Rhoda Métraux. *International Journal of Social Psychiatry*, vol. 6
(1960), p. 225-31.
This paper attempts to relate the individual responses that Abel discusses in
'Differential responses to projective testing in a negro peasant community: Montserrat,
B.W.I.' (q.v.) to a cultural context in which modernization and personal independence
are important values, and to a society in continuous flux. In this environment many
persons have experiences that are not shared by others and which ongoing change
makes difficult for them to interpret.

184 **Mental health and cross-cultural evaluations.**
Theodora M. Abel. *International Mental Health Research Newsletter*,
vol. 4, no. 3-4 (1962), p. 1-5.
This article interprets projective tests administered to a group of Montserrat rural
village dwellers in 1954. The author, a psychiatrist, concludes that the independence
that characterizes values and behaviour in Montserrat is a defence against strong
dependency needs that may be rooted in the uncertainties of economic life on the
island. Abel concludes with suggestions for comparative, cross-cultural research on the
personality characteristics and mental health of similar groups in different places.

185 **Normal and deviant behaviour in a peasant community.**
Rhoda Métraux, Theodora M. Abel. *American Journal of Orthopsychiatry*, vol. 27 (1957), p. 167-84.

This paper is based on the collaboration of a cultural anthropologist (Métraux) and a clinical psychologist (Abel). Their research, using Rorschach tests on Montserrat villagers, showed little deviant behaviour, whether defined psychologically or socially. Both the psychological and anthropological interpretations of the Rorschach data indicated regularities in the personalities of rural Montserrat dwellers.

Migration

186 **Emigration and depopulation.**
David Lowenthal, Lambros Comitas. *Geographical Review*, vol. 52, no. 2 (1962), p. 195-210.

The authors discuss and illustrate the effect of emigration on the sending country, using Montserrat as one of two case studies. Montserrat, a society dependent on remittances that emigrants living abroad send back home, lost twenty-one per cent of its population to emigration between 1939 and 1960. Young people leave because the economy cannot support them, yet the costs of depopulation are also great: per capita costs of services rise, there are shortages of skilled personnel, class divisions are intensified as the middle class departs and outside aid becomes essential. Although thirty years have passed since the article was written, the situation has not changed.

187 **The implications of migration for sending societies: some theoretical considerations.**
Stuart B. Philpott. In: *Migration and anthropology.* Edited by Robert F. Spencer. Seattle, Washington: University of Washington Press, 1970, p. 9-20.

The author uses his research in Montserrat to develop hypotheses about the effects that large-scale emigration will have on the sending societies. The remittances that emigrants abroad send home are important to the economy of the sending society, and make it possible for families to educate their children and purchase land.

188 **Mass migration in Montserrat.**
Stuart B. Philpott. PhD thesis, University of London, 1971. 349p.

Although Philpott was not the first anthropologist to do research in Montserrat, he was the first to undertake a comprehensive field study based on long residence. This thesis includes chapters on history, social organization and economy, and develops the idea that large-scale emigration has helped to shape Montserratian society.

189 **Remittance obligations: social networks and choice among Montserratian migrants in Britain.**
Stuart B. Philpott. *Man*, vol. 3 (1968), p. 465-76.
The author worked among Montserratian residents in London, and discovered that a network of relationships in the emigrant community exerted social pressure on its members to send money back home to families in Montserrat.

190 **Return migration and remittances: developing a Caribbean perspective.**
William F. Stinner, Klaus de Albuquerque, Roy S. Bryce-Laporte.
Washington DC: Research Institute on Immigration and Ethnic Studies, Smithsonian Institution, 1982. 322p. bibliog.
This collection of papers has two themes: remittances sent home by emigrants abroad, and return of these emigrants to their original homes. The essays by Hymie Rubenstein, Bonham Richardson, Rosemary Brana-Shute and Gary Brana-Shute both refer to Montserrat and enhance our understanding of migration in Montserrat by placing it in a larger economic, regional and world context.

West Indian migration: the Montserrat case.
See item no. 9.

Economic problems of the smaller West Indian islands.
See item no. 220.

The economy of Montserrat: a national accounts study.
See item no. 221.

Health and Medicine

191 **Arthropod-borne encephalitis viruses in the West Indies area, Part VIII: a serological survey of Montserrat.**
E. S. Tikasingh, L. Spence, A. H. Jonkers, A. E. Green. *West Indian Medical Journal*, vol. 15, no. 2 (1966), p. 112-17.

Blood samples from the Montserrat population were analysed in order to determine the presence of viruses causing encephalitis (brain inflammation).

192 **Hemoglobin levels in West Indian antenatals.**
W. K. Simmons, H. Wynter. *West Indian Medical Journal*, vol. 36, no. 4 (1987), p. 216-24.

Anaemia in pregnancy is a widespread health problem in the Commonwealth Caribbean. The authors compared the haemoglobin levels of pregnant women from Antigua and Montserrat with clinical records of haemoglobin levels from Jamaica, and found them lower. The authors conclude that treatment could raise the haemoglobin levels of other Commonwealth Caribbean pregnant women to those of Jamaican women, since the women all share the same ethnic background and a genetic factor in their anaemia may therefore be discounted.

193 **The incidence of cutaneous *larva migrans* in Montserrat, Leeward Islands, West Indies.**
C. P. Lee, L. J. Bishop. *West Indian Medical Journal*, vol. 37, no. 1 (1988), p. 22-24.

Larva migrans, or creeping eruption, is a skin disorder in human beings caused by the larvae of several species of hookworm that penetrate and move in the skin instead of entering the intestine, which is more usual behaviour. *Larva migrans* is a health hazard wherever hookworm in dogs, cats and cattle is common and where climate and soil conditions favour the survival of filariform larvae.

194   **An island-wide survey for helminth parasites in Montserrat, West Indies.**
        M. S. Wong, L. L. Lewis, D. A. P. Bundy. *West Indian Medical Journal*, vol. 37 no. 24 (1988), supplement.
A sample of the Montserrat population was tested for helminth parasite infections in 1986. The researchers discovered that slightly over fifteen per cent of the sample showed helminthic infection, especially *Trichuris trichiura*, which is prevalent among children aged two to sixteen.

195   **Nutritional status of young children in the English-speaking Caribbean.**
        M. Gueri. *Cajanus*, vol. 10, no. 5 (1977), 267-81.
This paper synthesizes a variety of different research projects carried out from 1970 to 1977. The author found that twenty-five to fifty per cent of children under the age of five were underweight. Tables display the data by island, age, birth weight, death rates, hospital admissions and body weight for age.

196   **Parasitic diseases in the Caribbean in 1982: intestinal parasites.**
        World Health Organization. *Weekly Epidemiological Record*, vol 59, no. 18 (1984), p. 133-36.
A total of 436 residents of three villages in Montserrat were tested for schistosomiasis (*Schistosoma mansoni*), and thirty-five per cent were found to be infected. The highest rate of infection occurred in the fifteen to twenty-five year-old age group.

197   **The presence of *Schistosoma mansoni* in Montserrat, Leeward Islands, West Indies.**
        E. S. Tikasingh, E. S. Wooding. *Journal of Tropical Medicine and Hygiene*, vol. 85, no. 1 (1982), p. 41-44.
In 1978, 132 persons in two Montserrat villages were tested for schistosomiasis infection. Fourteen per cent carried schistosome eggs, for which treatment was recommended.

198   **The role of the nurse in the past – flashback: Montserrat.**
        Ella Luty. *Jamaica Nurse*, vol. 8, no. 2 (1968), p. 10.
A brief memoir of the author's nursing experience in Montserrat and its relationship to the evolution of nursing in the Caribbean.

199   **Schistosomiasis and its intermediate hosts in the Lesser Antillean islands of the Caribbean.**
        M. A. Prentice. *Bulletin of the Pan-American Health Organization*, vol. 14, no. 3 (1980), p. 258-68.
This article examines the incidence of schistosomiasis and the status of host snails in a range of Lesser Antillean islands. In Montserrat the incidence of the disease was low in 1980, but there is now increasing danger of infection.

Health and Medicine

200 **Tuberculosis in Montserrat.**
   Philip Norman Griffin. *Caribbean Medical Journal*, vol. 22, no. 1-4
   (1960), p. 114-15.
This brief note reports on the incidence of tuberculosis in Montserrat and the measures
employed against it.

201 **Weaning practices from Guiana, rural Trinidad (Fishing Pond Village),**
   Grenada, Montserrat and Antigua.
   J. Michael Gurney. *West Indian Medical Journal*, vol. 20, no. 3
   (1972), p. 227-28.
This brief summary and synthesis of weaning practices in the West Indies was
abstracted from studies done in each location by students of community nutrition. The
Montserrat study had been done by Doris E. Bramble in 1969. Although there is much
individual variation in feeding practices, most babies in Montserrat are being given
solid foods by the end of their first year.

The African exchange: toward a biological history of black people.
See item no. 128.

Cajanus.
See item no. 314.

Politics, Law and Government

Local government, local politics and colonial status

202 **The future of the British Caribbean dependencies.**
Tony Thorndike. *Journal of Interamerican Studies and World Affairs*,
vol. 31 (1989), p. 117-40.
Six small British dependencies remain in the Caribbean region, among them
Montserrat, and the people of each have steadfastly refused independence. The author
shows that the reasons for their refusal of independence include small size, small
population, a perception of insecurity and economic vulnerability. Montserrat,
however, he thinks is capable of economic expansion through its participation in
CARICOM, the Caribbean regional organization for economic cooperation. He
concludes by considering alternatives to both dependency status and full independence.
These include associated statehood, a protected status and integration into an already
existing state.

203 **Montserrat the last English colony? Prospects for independence. Part I
and Part II.**
Howard A. Fergus. *Bulletin of Eastern Caribbean Affairs*, vol. 4, no.
3 (July-August 1978), p. 15-23; vol. 4, no. 4 (September-October 1978),
p. 23-28.
Fergus argues that political independence does not require prior economic independence; rather, the greater autonomy and altered political economy that independence
brings will make economic stability more achievable. Nevertheless, two important
factors hinder the achievement of independence: the people are insecure and hold
unconsidered attitudes toward independence, and the island functions much as a self-
governing territory despite the presence of a British governor. These factors persuaded
a United Nations mission to recommend no change in Montserrat's colonial status.
Additional arguments against independence include Montserrat's small size, the reality

of economic dependence and opposition of a conservative middle class. Fergus points out that other arguments favour independence, including the necessity for ending colonialism, a people's right of self-determination, and Montserrat's needs for political and economic change and for autonomous dealings with the entire Caribbean community.

204 **Personalities in Montserratian politics: comments on the 1983 general elections.**
Howard A. Fergus. *Bulletin of Eastern Caribbean Affairs*, vol. 10 (2), p. 26-34.

The 1983 election was a contest among three parties, the Peoples' Liberation Movement, the Progressive Democratic Party and the United National Front. Fergus argues that personalities rather than issues attract votes. He discusses three contemporary political leaders, explores the way their personalities affected elections, and points out that no successful candidates had university educations and all had autocratic styles. At the same time the electorate has not maintained any predictable party alignments. These features of Montserrat politics have developed since 1952, when W. H. Bramble, a local black labour leader of the Progressive Democratic Party, upset the merchant-planter oligarchy for the first time.

205 **Rule Britannia: politics in British Montserrat.**
Howard A. Fergus. Plymouth, Montserrat: University Centre of the West Indies, 1985. 115p.

This book includes chapters on elections, electoral behaviour, women in politics, politics and personalities, the constitution, and the debate on independence. The author, who favours independence, discusses the factors that have led Montserratian politics into a conservative, Anglophile and ultimately damaging stance on independence. Fergus also provides a history of election results from 1952 to 1983, and information on candidates and British administrators.

206 **Statement on Montserrat.**
Organization of Eastern Caribbean States, Sixteenth Meeting, November 23-24, 1989. *Bulletin of Eastern Caribbean Affairs*, vol. 15, no. 4-5 (1989), p. 55-56.

This statement was prepared by the heads of government of the member countries of the OECS in order to protest a new constitutional order to be imposed by Great Britain on Montserrat in December 1989. The new order is considered retrogressive in that it restricts the authority of the elected government and restores to the British governing officer appointed by Great Britain 'a degree of autocratic power that smacks of the worst forms of colonialism' (p. 55). The OECS called upon the British Government to reconsider its intentions and ensure the rights of self-determination of the Montserratian people.

207 **Team management and development in Montserrat and Anguilla.**
J. E. Kersell. *Public Administration and Development*, vol. 10 (1990),
p. 81-91.

Montserrat and Anguilla, British colonies still remaining in the Caribbean, have
departed from British constitutional and political traditions in the practice of team
management in government administration. Team management techniques in government include reciprocity, trust, collective agreement and confidentiality. These
techniques visibly improve effectiveness, consensus, productivity and job satisfaction.
Nevertheless, newer public servants are often frustrated in their efforts at team
management by the reluctance of older public servants who have been trained for
hierarchical relations.

208 **William Henry Bramble: his life and times.**
Howard A. Fergus. Plymouth, Montserrat: University Centre,
University of the West Indies, 1983. 118p.

This biography of the first Montserratian chief minister of Montserrat was written by a
Montserratian historian of the faculty of the University of the West Indies centre in
Montserrat. Bramble began his political career in the late 1930s as a union activist. He
became the spokesperson for the poor, the landless and the working class of the island.
He began his term as chief minister in 1960 and retained that office until 1970.

Law

209 **Acts of Assembly, passed in the island of Montserrat; from 1668 to 1740,
inclusive.**
Montserrat Assembly. London: Lords Commissioners of Trade and
Plantations, 1740.

This is a chronological list, printed by John Baskett, of all the laws that were passed by
the legislature of Montserrat and approved by the Commission of Trade and
Plantations, the royally appointed board that dealt with colonial affairs.

210 **Commissioners' report on justice: Antigua, Montserrat, Nevis,
St. Christopher, and the Virgin Islands, general conclusions.**
Commission of Inquiry into the Administration of Civil and Criminal
Justice in the West Indies. London: House of Commons, 1826. 2 vols.

The Commission of Inquiry into the laws, courts, and administration of justice in the
West Indies travelled through the British Caribbean colonies in 1823. The
commissioners were especially concerned with the treatment and legal rights of slaves
and free people of colour, and with the administration and practice of the courts.
Montserrat's record on these matters was abysmal: the tiny size of the white oligarchy
could not supply personnel for the competent and just operation of the court system,
the legislature refused to admit the rights of free persons of colour to participate in
juries or to vote, and the amelioration of slave conditions was backward (vol. 2,
p. 30-38).

211 **The early laws of Montserrat (1668-1680): the legal schema of a slave society.**
Howard A. Fergus. *Caribbean Quarterly*, vol. 24 (1978), p. 34-43.

Fergus has analysed the laws passed in Montserrat during the period when a slave labour force was replacing an indentured servant labour force. The kinds of legislation passed show us the nature of the society founded on slavery during its formative period.

212 **Montserrat code of laws: from 1668, to 1788.**
Council and Assembly of His Majesty's Island of Montserrat.
London: J. Anderson, 1790. 87p.

This is a chronological list of all the laws passed by the Montserrat Council and the Montserrat Assembly from 1668 to 1788. It supplements and revises the *Acts of Assembly . . . 1668-1740* (q.v.).

213 **Montserrat: consolidated index of statutes and subsidiary legislation to 1st January 1986.**
Government of Montserrat.   Holmes Beach, Florida: William Gaunt & Sons, 1986. 78p.

Just as its title indicates, this compilation is an index to all legislation passed in Montserrat up to 1986.

214 **The revised laws of Montserrat.**
Cecil P. Lewis.   London: Waterloo & Sons Ltd., 1965. 9 vols.

This is the complete and official compendium of Montserrat law as of the publication date, 1965, and comprises 5,524 pages.

215 **Tourist divorces and the abuse of a small state's legal system: the Montserrat matrimonial causes for foreigners ordinance, 1978.**
K. W. Patchett, J. R. Young.   *American Journal of Law*, vol. 30, no. 4 (1982), p. 654-77.

In April 1978 a law was passed in Montserrat that enabled short-term visitors to obtain a divorce and to remarry easily. This law was offered as a service to develop tourism, following the practices of Haiti and the Dominican Republic, but was repealed less than a year later. This article analyses the Montserratian law and relates it to three larger legal issues: the 'drafting of complex legislation in states with limited legal resources', (p. 655); the transfer of legal concepts from one system into another, and the implications of quick divorce laws for international law.

Bulletin of Eastern Caribbean Affairs.
See item no. 313.

Caribbean Monthly Bulletin.
See item no. 323.

Biographical dictionary of Latin American and Caribbean political leaders.
See item no. 332.

Political parties of the Americas.
See item no. 340.

South America, Central America, and the Caribbean.
See item no. 341.

Economy

216 **Agriculture and tourism essential.**
Caribbean and West Indies Chronicle, no. 1551 (1979), p. 17-18.
Tourism and agriculture are the largest employers in Montserrat. The government has therefore decided to develop tourism and to establish an Agricultural Development Authority to plan programmes of commercial crop and dairy production that will make Montserrat self-sufficient in food.

217 **Budget: Montserrat.**
Caricom Perspective, no. 37 (Jan.-Mar. 1987), p. 46.
This brief résumé of the 1987 budget explains its goals and major features, including estimated income and expense and a proposal for new airport facilities (on which construction in fact began in 1990). The budget provides for government funds to aid in home ownership as part of a long-term goal of raising the Montserratian standard of living.

218 **Development plan, 1966-1970.**
Government of Montserrat. Bridgetown, Barbados: Advocate, 1966.
93p.
Describes the government plan for public sector development of tourism and agriculture. The plan calls for development of residential tourism and a cruise port, and the replacement of subsistence cultivation by commercial market gardening and horticulture.

219 **Economic problems of the Leeward and Windward Islands.**
Carleen O'Loughlin. *Social Scientist*, vol 1, no. 3-4 (1963-64), p. 8-21.
Summarizes the economic problems of the small islands of the Lesser Antilles. These include underemployment, economic stagnation and the consequent persistent flow of emigrants. Montserrat especially exemplifies these problems.

220 Economic problems of the smaller West Indian islands.
Carleen O'Loughlin. *Social and Economic Studies*, vol. 11, no. 1 (1962), p. 44-56.

The author focuses on West Indian economies that had not seen any increase in gross domestic product in the five years previous to 1961. She discusses Montserrat in detail because Montserrat represents the potential condition of other small territories in the Lesser Antilles, where lack of employment often results in large numbers of emigrants. Thus the potential labour force, upon which any possible economic development depends, is depleted and reviving the economy is rendered ever more difficult.

221 The economy of Montserrat: a national accounts study.
Carleen O'Loughlin. *Social and Economic Studies*, vol. 8 (1959), p. 147-78.

O'Loughlin surveys Montserrat's agriculture, industries, public finances, rents, household income, and expenses of government. She shows how Montserrat is exemplary of the special economic problems of small islands: small population and limited market; cost and difficulties of export production; need for external transport without volume to attract carriers; high cost of imports; and shortages of goods and trained personnel. In addition, Montserrat has particular problems. The coastline offers little harbourage, and there are few attractive sand beaches to stimulate tourism. Cultivation is difficult because of slope, erosion, recurrent droughts and uneven distribution of rainfall. Emigration is an understandable consequence of an economy that provides minimally, yet emigration exacerbates the problems of personnel and demographic structure.

222 Loan fees – now you see them, now you don't.
Douglas Frantz. *Los Angeles Times*, vol. 108 (April 16, 1989), p. 7, section IV.

This report results from an investigation of frauds practised by private banks located in Montserrat. Montserrat was, until 1989, a haven for foreign-owned 'offshore' banks that engaged in money-laundering and other illegal practices. The inability of Montserrat's local government to control the activities of international banks led to the unilateral and unpopular decision on the part of Great Britain to expand its colonial oversight on the island.

223 Montserrat: economic survey projections.
British Development Division in the Caribbean. Barbados: British Development Division in the Caribbean, 1967. 28p.

This survey analyses the private sector economy and the areas of need for British aid. It shows that economic growth in Montserrat from 1961 to 1965 took place in housing construction and expanding tourism. It departs from the Montserrat Government's *Development plan, 1966-1970* (q.v.) in that it projects only a precarious future for commercial agriculture.

224 Montserrat: the economy.
Caribbean Update, (May 1989), p. 14-15.

This article reports on the state of the Montserrat economy and economic climate during the period of 1989 in which banking frauds were uncovered.

Economy

225 **On tiny isle of 300 banks, enter Scotland Yard.**
Joseph B. Treaster. *New York Times*, vol. 138 (July 27, 1989), p. A4
and A8.
Considers the involvement of banks located in Montserrat in international banking
frauds and money-laundering schemes.

226 **Proclamation under the Trade Act of 1974.**
United States. Washington DC: US Government Printing Office,
1982.
This proclamation notifies all the members of the Caribbean Common Market –
Montserrat, Antigua and Barbuda, Barbados, Belize, Dominica, Grenada, Guyana,
Jamaica, St. Kitts-Nevis, St. Lucia, St. Vincent and the Grenadines, and Trinidad and
Tobago – that the United States will consider them as a single country for the purposes
of trade preferences.

227 **Report on private sector strategy for the Regional Development Office in
the Caribbean.**
Washington, DC: Agency for International Development, 1988. 54p.
This report analyses the prospects for development by means of private enterprise in
the eastern Caribbean, including Montserrat. The small states of the eastern Caribbean
must work within common constraints: lack of collateral security and subsequent
difficulties in obtaining financing; inexperience with private enterprise and inadequate
government policy; and the problems of scale in microstates. The report assesses
performance of agriculture, tourism and manufacturing in these states and outlines a
strategy for AID programmes to encourage private sector development in the region.

228 **Report on the draft physical development plan for Montserrat, West
Indies.**
S. I. D. McKee. Plymouth, Monserrat: Government Printery, 1966.
47p. maps.
The author explains that the economic expansion in Montserrat during the 1960s was
due wholly to the construction of housing by foreign residents and the sale of coastal
lands for real estate development. Therefore a land use and zoning plan is necessary to
preserve good agricultural land, to slow down the sale of land to foreigners, to
stimulate conservation of land resources, and to stimulate true economic expansion
from within. Since most development voices in the 1960s called for continued
residential tourism, and continue to call for tourism development, this single advocate
for a comprehensive land use and zoning plan that would preserve Montserrat's
resources is a worthwhile, if unheeded, alternative.

229 **Select technological issues in agro-industry.**
J. A. Whitehead. *Social and Economic Studies*, vol. 28, no. 1 (1979),
p. 139-88.
This study deals with the food-processing activities in Montserrat, Barbados,
Dominica, St. Lucia and St. Kitts-Nevis. It concludes that the development of food-
processing industries in these islands requires wider choices of technology and more
facilities for research and training. The author believes that local food-processing
industries can increase their output and thus their contribution to local and regional
employment and economy.

230 **Small island economies.**
DeLisle Worrell. New York: Praeger, 1987. 289p.
The author, director of economic research at the Central Bank of Barbados, deals with the special economic problems that arise in tiny island states. Chapter 7 (p. 163-79) includes a discussion of Montserrat, where a tourist expansion in the 1970s was not sustained through the early 1980s, and which depends on budget grants from the United Kingdom.

231 **Stormy weather.**
The Economist, vol. 313, no. 7632 (December 9, 1989), p. 41.
Although hurricane Hugo, which devastated Montserrat in September 1989, temporarily pushed aside concern with Montserrat's international banking frauds of that year, further news about these frauds later surfaced. This report deals with the issuing of banking licences in Montserrat and its link with Montserratian politics.

Government of Montserrrat statistical digest.
See item no. 303.

National accounts statistics, 1975-1982.
See item no. 304.

Overseas trade report.
See item no. 305.

Caribbean Dateline.
See item no. 317.

Caribbean Economic Almanac.
See item no. 319.

Caribbean Insight.
See item no. 322.

Caribbean Monthly Bulletin.
See item no. 323.

Caribbean Update.
See item no. 329.

Caricom Perspective.
See item no. 330.

South America, Central America, and the Caribbean.
See item no. 341.

Agriculture and Soils

Soils

232 **The agricultural soils of Montserrat.**
  F. Hardy, G. Rodrigues, W. R. E. Nanton. Trinidad: Imperial
  College of Tropical Agriculture, 1949. 68p. map. (Studies in West
  Indian Soils, XI).
An excellent source not only on the soils of Montserrat, but on the physiography and
land use pattern of the island.

233 **Soil and land-use survey no. 22: Montserrat.**
  D. M. Lang. Trinidad: Regional Research Centre, University of the
  West Indies, 1967. 64p. maps.
This definitive field survey of Montserrat's soils includes descriptions of soil types and
their origins, discussions of land uses and their suitability to soil types, recommenda-
tions about agriculture, and soil and land use maps in colour.

234 **Soil productivity in the British Caribbean region.**
  F. Hardy. *Tropical Agriculture*, vol. 28, no. 1-6 (1951), p. 3-25.
A review article which summarizes and systematizes research on soil productivity in the
British Caribbean as of 1950. It classifies soil types, discusses their physical features
and agricultural usefulness, and relates them to vegetation, physiography and geology.
The article supplies a regional context for understanding the soils and agricultural
problems of Montserrat.

235 **The soils of Montserrat.**
F. Hardy. *West Indian Bulletin*, vol. 19 (1922), p.189-213.
This article describes the different soils of Montserrat, their distribution, their physical properties and structure, and the relationship of soil types and structure to the failure of commercial lime tree cultivation on the island.

236 **The soils of Montserrat.**
Francis Watts, H. A. Tempany. *West Indian Bulletin*, vol. 6 (1906), p. 263-84.
Soil samples were taken from various parts of the island and analysed for fertility factors, especially potash, phosphates, nitrogen and carbonates. The authors conclude the soils are generally fertile, easily worked, not deficient in nutrients and not in need of any artificial fertilizer. They are suitable for a variety of crops, among which limes, cacao, Sea Island cotton and vegetables are recommended.

Small farming and food production

237 **Effects of applied N, P and K fertilizers on the chemical composition of the ear-leaf of maize (*Zea mays* L.) in field trials in the eastern Caribbean. Further studies on the evaluation and calibration of soil analysis methods for N, P, and K in the Eastern Caribbean.**
D. Walmsley, St. Clair M. Ford. *Tropical Agriculture*, vol. 53, no. 4 (1976), p. 273-80; p. 281-91.
These two articles are based on field research and planned to determine whether information on the amounts of nitrogen, phosphorus and potassium already in soils could predict the response of crops to added fertilizers. Maize was tested in Montserrat, Antigua, Dominica and St. Kitts. The research determined the critical amounts of N, P and K below which crops could be expected to show an improvement with the addition of fertilizer, but above which fertilizer would not make a difference. Thus the testing of soils for these nutrients can help cultivators of Montserrat determine whether the addition of fertilizer will improve their crop yields.

238 **Erosion hazard and farming systems in the Caribbean countries.**
N. Ahmad. In: *Soil conservation and management in the humid tropics.* Edited by D. J. Greenland, R. Lal. Chichester, England: John Wiley & Sons, 1977. p. 241-49.
This article assesses the management of soil erosion in systems of shifting cultivation on sloped land in the Caribbean. The shifting cultivators of Montserrat's mountain slopes manage soil and drainage by hoeing raised horizontal ridges across their fields.

Agriculture and Soils. Small farming and food production

239   **A land use plan for Trants Estate, Montserrat.**
      M. J. Wilson, N. McD. W. Meade.   Plymouth, Montserrat:
      Department of Agriculture, 1973. 51p. maps.
The authors devised a plan for land use and the allotment of small farms to farmers on
the former Trants Estate. The report includes information on the farms, farmers, farm
production and government plans for farm assistance and small plot ownership.

240   **Migration and rural development in the Caribbean.**
      Janet D. Momsen.   *Tijdschrift voor Economische en Sociale Geografie*,
      vol 77, no. 1, p. 50-58.
The author surveyed small farmers in Montserrat, Nevis and St. Lucia to discover
whether the migration experience affected small plot cultivation. She found that
returned migrant cultivators were not associated with farming innovations, often had
negative attitudes toward farming and often farmed less productively. Further,
returned migrants were more likely than others to produce export cash crops on their
small plots.

241   **The new Otway farms: a land use plan for the Otway Estate,
      Montserrat.**
      M. J. Wilson.   Plymouth, Montserrat: Department of Agriculture,
      1972. 63p. maps.
Late in 1972, 135 farmers received land allotments in a new settlement scheme on the
former Otway Estate, near Plymouth. Nearly a quarter of the farmers engaged in
commercial vegetable production. This report summarizes the features of the new
farms, the farmers and their farm production. It describes the government plan for
farm ownership and the provision of irrigation and assistance to farmers.

242   **Planned production programme, Montserrat, W.I.**
      R. Nurden.   *Tropical Agriculture*, vol. 64, no. 1 (1987), p. 72-73.
In 1986 the Montserrat Ministry of Agriculture organized a Production Co-ordination
Unit (PCU) to disseminate production and marketing information to small farmers,
and to send extension officers to assist small farmers on their plots. The PCU was
staffed by agronomists sent by the US Peace Corps and the British Voluntary Service
Overseas.

243   **A profile of small farming in Antigua, Montserrat, and Grenada.**
      Faculty of Agriculture, University of the West Indies, St. Augustine,
      Trinidad.   Barbados: Caribbean Agricultural Research and
      Development Institute, 1980. 54p. (Farm Systems Database Series,
      no. 3).
This report is the last of a series based on a survey of six territories in the eastern
Caribbean. The entire research effort was intended to provide information that would
help to develop improvements in small farming, and to create a database of social and
economic information related to small farmers. This report provides the following
information about Montserrat small farms: sizes of farm holdings, age distribution of
farmers, farm family incomes, locations of holdings, livestock census and livestock
numbers per holding, farming practices and marketing. The research also involved
surveying farmers about their household economies, decision-making, nutrition and

attitudes about education, health care, occupational preferences and desires concerning their children's futures.

244 **Small farming in the less developed countries of the Caribbean.**
C. Bourne, C. C. Weir. Barbados: Caribbean Development Bank, 1980. 335p.

The Caribbean Development Bank commissioned a survey of small farming that included detailed field studies of small farms in Montserrat, Dominica and St. Vincent. Chapter 6 of the final report is devoted to Montserrat (p. 201-30). The authors argue that small farming is central to the agricultural development of Montserrat and that measures are necessary to ensure its success. These incude improved inter-island transport for produce, a workable pricing policy, and reliable supplies of fertilizer and mechanized tools at prices small farmers can afford.

245 **Subsistence cultivation in the Caribbean.**
Riva Berleant-Schiller, Lydia Mihelic Pulsipher. *Nieuwe West-Indische Gids/New West Indian Guide*, vol. 60, no. 1-2 (1986), p. 1-40.

Uses the results of research carried out in Montserrat and Barbuda to develop hypotheses about the core features of pan-Caribbean small-plot cultivation, a central characteristic of culture, land use and household economy everywhere in the Caribbean. The article succinctly describes island topography and graded environmental zones based on elevation, moisture and vegetation. It analyses crop complexes and gardening practices in detail, and draws comparisons between the crops and gardens of the Caribbean and of other areas in the American tropics. It includes maps and descriptions of actual food gardens in Montserrat and Barbuda and a comprehensive bibliography of Caribbean small-plot cultivation.

Commodities

246 **The Caribbean Sea Island Cotton Co.**
Caribbean Update, (January 1990), p. 4.

The cotton production and marketing company formed by the islands of Montserrat, Antigua and Barbados in December 1989 has acquired a ginnery for its product, located in Barbados.

247 **Caribbean sea island cotton venture formed.**
Financial Times, (December 7 1989), p. 36.

The Caribbean Sea Island Cotton Company has been formed by Montserrat, Antigua and Barbados to revive the sea island cotton industry in those islands and to produce and market a cotton of high quality.

248 **Cotton selection in Montserrat. The manner of cross-pollination of cotton in Montserrat. Sakellarides cotton in Montserrat.**
W. Robson. *West Indian Bulletin*, vol. 13 (1913), p. 22-28.
Three consecutive brief articles treat problems in cotton culture at a time when British colonial policy promoted cotton production in the Leeward Islands Colony.

249 **Limes in Montserrat: a project appraisal.**
M. Upton. Reading, Pennsylvania: University of Reading Department of Agricultural Economics, 1971. 69p.
Commercial lime production was first initiated in Montserrat in the mid-nineteenth century and has had its periods of favour and disfavour since then. The lime project of 1970 followed Montserrat's development plans of the late sixties, which emphasized commercial crop production. This report assesses the lime project.

250 **Montserrat cotton industry enquiry report.**
Cyril G. Beasley, Swithin A. Schouten. Plymouth, Montserrat: Government of Montserrat, 1954. 66p.
This report covers much more than the Montserrat cotton industry, which was economically important in the 1950s, when about thirty per cent of all cultivated land was in cotton. Even though the product was a fine, strong, long staple fibre, the market was limited and the price was dropping. Thus the report assesses the Montserrat peasant economy and its possible future. It includes information on land distribution and tenure, household economy and economic alternatives to cotton production. It is, however, extremely ethnocentric in its descriptions of Montserrat rural life and unsympathetic to local values and ways of life. It is therefore a document that exemplifies a metropolitan attitude of superiority and the application of fixed metropolitan standards to a colonized land and people. It concludes that although Montserratian cotton is of high quality and economically significant in Montserrat, it is an overly specialized product insignificant to the world cotton industry.

251 **Montserrat's days of lime and cotton.**
Howard A. Fergus. *Caribbean Quarterly*, vol. 28, no. 3 (1982), p. 10-18.
This article is a brief history of cotton and lime production in Montserrat that analyses the relationship of production to labour supply, emigration and the real estate boom of the 1960s. Fergus concludes that there is still a possibility that a return to cotton and lime production might alleviate Montserrat's economic problems.

252 **Notes on the thymol content of horse-mint (*Monarda punctata* and ajowan seed (*Carum copticum*).**
A. E. Collens. *West India Bulletin*, vol 17, no. 1 (1918), p. 50-55.
The search for a satisfactory cash crop for Montserrat is perennial. Both horse-mint and ajowan produce an aromatic oil, thymol, that is used in manufacturing drugs and cosmetics. Although the author concludes from his analyses of product quality and world market that both crops could be profitably grown in Montserrat, he warns that

commodity markets change. Neither plant has ever become an economically important export crop in Montserrat.

253 **Progress of the sea island cotton industry in the West Indies.**
Thomas Thornton. *West India Bulletin*, vol. 9, no. 3 (1908), p. 215-19.
Includes assessment of Montserrat's cotton production during a period when British government policy promoted cotton in the Caribbean colonies.

254 **Report on Montserrat, 1929-1931.**
Imperial College of Tropical Agriculture. Trinidad: Imperial College of Tropical Agriculture, 1932. 32p.
This report on commercial agriculture in Montserrat is useful for its information on attempts to revive the lime industry that had been established in the second half of the nineteenth century and devastated by disease and hurricane by 1899. Once again, however, lime trees planted in 1928 were destroyed by a hurricane that year, and apparently successful production in 1930 and 1931 was halted by disease.

Pests and diseases

255 **The economic impact of tomato diseases in Montserrat.**
P. Crill, P. A. J. Arthurton, R. Phelps. *Plant Disease Reporter*, vol. 56, no. 9 (1972), p. 817-19.
The authors' survey of tomato fields and external disease symptoms on the island indicated the presence of the tobacco mosaic virus and the potato virus Y in tomatoes, among other infections. Attention to the health of plants is necessary for the protection of the commercial tomato crop.Root-knot nematodes cause the greatest crop loss.

256 **Epidemiological studies of heartwater in the Caribbean.**
M. J. Burridge, N. Barre, N. Birnie, E. F. Camus, G. Uilenberg. *Proceedings of the 13th World Congress on Diseases of Cattle*, vol. 1 (1984), p. 542-46.
The authors surveyed herds of cattle, sheep and goats throughout the Caribbean for the occurrence of *Amblyomma* ticks. *A. variegatum* was found to occur widely in Montserrat.

257 **Hot pepper mosaic: an important disease in the West Indies.**
O. S. Lloyd Thomas. *Tropical Pest Management*, vol. 28, no. 1 (1982), p. 88-89.
Montserrat is an important commercial producer of hot peppers (*Capsicum frutescens*), which earns twenty-four per cent of Montserrat's export income. The Montserrat Ministry of Agriculture surveyed the prevalence of hot pepper mosaic, a plant virus

infection, by sampling peppers from all pepper farms. The survey showed that twenty-five per cent of the crop was infected, with the most severe occurrence in the east and central parts of the island.

258 **Occurrence of plant parasitic nematodes in Montserrat, West Indies.**
C. W. D. Brathwaite. *FAO Plant Protection Bulletin*, vol. 22, no. 3 (1974), p. 69-71.

Research undertaken in 1972 showed that all commercially important vegetable crops in Montserrat were infested with fourteen different genera of nematode, and suggests that these parasites contributed to recent poor crop yields.

259 **An outbreak of hot pepper mosaic disease in Montserrat.**
O. S. LLoyd Thomas. *FAO Plant Protection Bulletin*, vol. 28, no. 3 (1980), p. 117.

A note reporting the outbreak of a virus disease affecting the important commercial pepper crop on Montserrat. About forty-four per cent of the yield was lost.

260 **Pest and pesticide management in the Caribbean: vol. 3.**
Edited by J. L. Hammerton, J. L. Gooding. Bridgetown, Barbados: Consortium for International Crop Protection, 1981. 204p.

This is the third volume of proceedings of a meeting on agricultural pest control held in Barbados in 1980. It contains reports from sixteen Caribbean countries and territories. The paper on Montserrat considers the impact on agriculture and on public health of the use of pesticides and pest management.

261 **Plant parasitic nematode problems associated with vegetable production in the Leeward Islands.**
C. W. D. Brathwaite, R. H. Phelps, F. D. Bennett. In: *Proceedings of a symposium on the protection of horticultural crops in the Caribbean*. St. Augustine, Trinidad: University of the West Indies, 1974, p. 135-44.

Research on nematode infestations in Montserrat showed that tomato yields increased by fifty-five per cent when an anti-nematode pesticide, Nemagon, was added to the soil. The authors stress the need for nematode control in commercial vegetable crops in Montserrat and the Leewards.

262 **The probability of the spread of *Amblyomma variegatum* in the Caribbean.**
F. J. Alderink, E. Hunt McCauley. *Preventive Veterinary Medicine*, vol. 6, no. 4 (1988), p. 285-94.

Amblyomma variegatum is a tick that infests domestic grazing animals such as cattle and sheep. The authors estimate that this parasite will spread in the Caribbean at the rate of about one island a year. It is already found widely in Montserrat. The authors consider the history of the spread of closely related parasites, such as *A. americanum*, which did not arrive in Montserrat until 1980, even though it apparently entered the Caribbean at Guadeloupe in 1828.

263 **Report on the Antigua, Montserrat and St. Kitts-Nevis entomology programme 1975-1977.**
N. S. Irving. London: Centre for Overseas Pest Research, 1978. 55p.
This report describes the biology, behaviour and injuriousness of over twenty species of arthropod that attack crops. It examines the effects of insecticides and biological controls, and techniques for their application.

264 **Virus diseases of cultivated plants in Montserrat.**
O. S. Lloyd Thomas. *Tropical Pest Management*, vol. 27, no. 4 (1981), p. 461-64.
This report is the result of the first intensive survey of crop diseases ever undertaken on Montserrat. A range of virus diseases was discovered to affect squash, melons, peppers, tomatoes and beans. Cotton and sweet potatoes were found free of virus infections. The report includes a summary table of all the sap-transmissible plant virus diseases identified on the island.

Agricultural development

265 **Agricultural industries of Montserrat.**
Francis Watts. *West Indian Bulletin*, vol. 7, no. 1 (1906), p.1-15.
This is a report on agriculture in Montserrat in 1905 along with recommendations for its improvement. It is based on field research by Watts, who was at that time Agricultural Superintendent for the Leeward Islands. Montserratian agriculture in 1905 was made up principally of an impoverished sugar industry carried on under a sharecrop system; an export lime industry recently restored after its destruction by hurricane; and some cotton, livestock and cacao production. Cotton appeared to be developing as the most promising export crop. Significant for small plot cultivators was the papaya, which they 'milked' for its pharmaceutical extract, papain, and sold to the Montserrat Company, a local middleman enterprise.

266 **The agricultural industries of Montserrat.**
Francis Watts. *West Indian Bulletin*, vol 15, no. 1 (1916), p. 14-21.
This report was intended to bring Watts's 1906 report of the same title (q.v.) up to date. Cotton had indeed risen to first importance, as Watts had foreseen, but was suffering at the moment from depression induced by the First World War. Limes continued to improve, livestock export was good, but sugar showed no signs of recovery. Agricultural officers were experimenting with the commercial production of onions and bay leaf.

Agriculture and Soils. Agricultural development

267 **Establishment and management of improved pastures for small scale livestock production in Montserrat.**
R. E. Fletcher. In: *Pasture research and development in the eastern Caribbean.* St. John's, Antigua: Caribbean Agricultural Research and Development Institute (CARDI), 1986, p. 71-85.

A variety of forage crops and forage-legume combinations were grown on demonstration plots in Montserrat from 1983 to 1986. The plots showed that legume-forage combinations led to a decline in legume yield and weed problems. Pangola grass (*Digitaria decumbens*) showed the best drought resistance. The article also discusses other species of forage grasses, sowing and land preparation techniques, weed control, fertility maintenance, grassland management and dry-season feeding.

268 **External evaluation report on the Caribbean Agricultural Extension Project, Phase II.**
M. C. Alkin, K. A. Adams, M. Cuthbert, J. West. St. Paul, Minnesota: University of Minnesota Department of Agricultural Extension, 1984. 425p.

Phase II of the Caribbean Agricultural Extension Project aimed to provide training programmes and training for extension workers, to establish extension units, and to supply equipment for the conduct of agricultural demonstration schemes. This report evaluates individually the success of this project in each of the eight Caribbean states where it was carried out, including Montserrat.

269 **A partially annotated bibliography of agricultural development in the Caribbean region.**
Clarence Zuvekas. Washington, DC: Agency for International Development, Rural Development Division of the Bureau for Latin America and the Caribbean, 1978. 72p.

A useful bibliography of works related to agricultural development in the small islands of the English-speaking Caribbean, including Montserrat.

270 **Prospects for the development of livestock production in Montserrat and Antigua.**
P. A. J. Arthurton, F. Henry. In: *Proceedings of the tenth West Indies agricultural economics conference, vol. 2, workshop papers.* St. Augustine, Trinidad: Caribbean Agro-Economic Society, 1976, p. 186-96.

Since most of the meat eaten in Montserrat and Antigua is imported, developing commercial livestock production on these islands would reduce both imported inflation and the loss of foreign exchange. Expanded livestock production would require that land be available to those willing to invest in livestock, and that production methods be intensive.

70

271 **Report of post-harvest losses consultative meeting, Caribbean, July 1981.**
London: Commonwealth Secretariat, 1981. 2 vols.
A meeting to consider the post-harvest losses in the Caribbean was held at the University of the West Indies, Trinidad, in July, 1981. Volume 2, *Country Papers*, includes a report on Montserrat (p.131-34). It treats the general problems of and conditions that lead to the loss of food crops after harvest, especially among small farmers.

272 **Report on food production and the tourist industry in Montserrat.**
Janet Henshall Momsen. Calgary, Alberta: University of Calgary, 1973. 56p. maps.
This report, based on field research and a questionnaire, attempts to determine whether the growing of vegetables can be a workable commercial alternative to the shrinking sea-island cotton industry in Montserrat. The author considers the constraints on commercial vegetable production and marketing, and the economic characteristics of small producers. She concludes that the development of market gardens aimed at supplying the tourist industry can be a workable goal for small producers and can provide employment when the construction industry declines.

273 **Tropical departments of agriculture, with special reference to the West Indies.**
Francis Watts. *West Indian Bulletin*, vol. 18, no. 3 (1921), p. 101-33.
A review of the organization and activities of the departments of agriculture in what were, in 1921, British tropical colonies. The agricultural department of Montserrat is included in the discussion.

Ridged fields in Montserrat, West Indies.
See item no. 14.

Agriculture and tourism essential.
See item no. 216.

Development plan, 1966-1970.
See item no. 218.

Culture

Language

274 **The brogue that isn't.**
J. C. Wells. *Journal of the International Phonetics Association*, vol.
10, no. 1-2 (1980), p. 74-79.
The notion that Montserratians speak with an Irish brogue is widespread and
apparently uncontrollable. Nevertheless, it is pure myth. Wells's analysis of Montserrat
Creole is based on field research in Montserrat and among Montserratian residents in
the United Kingdom. Wells found that spoken Montserrat Creole has much in
common with all other Caribbean English-based creoles. These creoles share certain
phonological features with Southern Irish English, but none are peculiar to Montserrat
and it is not reasonable to propose that they are all influenced by spoken Irish English.
Further, rhythm and intonation are dissimilar, and there is nothing in Montserrat
Creole syntax or morphology, and only one word in Montserrat Creole vocabulary,
that can be attributed to Irish influence.

275 **General outlines of Creole English dialects in the British Caribbean.**
R. B. Le Page. *Orbis*, vol. 6, no. 2 (1957), p. 373-91; vol. 7, no. 1
(1958), p. 54-64.
Montserrat Creole is included in Le Page's general outline of the creole dialects spoken
throughout what is often called the Anglophone Caribbean.

276 **A linguistic perspective on the Caribbean.**
Mervyn C. Alleyne. In: *Caribbean contours*. Edited by Sidney W.
Mintz, Sally Price. Baltimore, Maryland: Johns Hopkins University
Press, 1985, p. 159-75.
This paper attempts to order the complexity of Caribbean language, especially the
creole tongues spoken in the region. The creole language of Montserrat is included in
the author's discussion.

277 **The socio-historical background to pidginization and creolization.**
Sidney W. Mintz.   In: *Pidginization and creolization of languages*.
Edited by Dell Hymes. London: Cambridge University Press, 1971,
p. 481-96.
This paper supplies a social and historical context, applicable to Montserrat, for the
development and use of creole languages in the Caribbean region.

278 **West Indians and their language.**
Peter A. Roberts.   London: Cambridge University Press, 1988. 215p.
This book discusses the varieties of English that are spoken in the Caribbean and is a
good, modern introduction to the topic. It includes a general discussion of Creole
English (often termed by other scholars 'English Creole') as well as a chapter on
linguistic variety within the Anglophone West Indies. The book also includes chapters
on the sources and cultural contexts of West Indian English Creole. There are many
tables showing vocabulary and usage that supply specific information about
Montserrat.

The myth of Irish origins

279 **Documents relating to the Irish in the West Indies.**
Aubrey Gwynn, S. J., M. A.   *Analecta Hibernia*, no. 4 (October
1932), p. 140-286.
This is a collection and transcription of manuscripts stored in the Public Record Office
of Dublin, the Public Record Office of London, the British Museum, and various other
archives in the West Indies, the United States, Spain, Portugal and France. It also
includes selected extracts from seventeenth-century printed sources. Many documents
and extracts refer specifically to Montserrat, and pages 183 to 273 should be carefully
examined by anyone interested in the Irish in Montserrat.

280 **The first Irish priests in the new world.**
Aubrey Gwynn, S. J..   *Studies: An Irish Quarterly of Letters*, 1932
(June), p. 212-28.
A great deal of unsupported nonsense can be found in print about the influence of
seventeenth-century Irish Catholic immigrants on Montserrat today. What few facts we
actually have about the earliest of these immigrants, who had arrived in Montserrat by
1634, can be found in this study.

281 **The 'Black Irish' of Montserrat.**
John C. Messenger.   *Eire-Ireland*, vol. 2 (1967), p. 27-40.
This article is based on six weeks of research in Montserrat and three weeks in libraries
in Ireland. However, the only two historical sources cited are T. Savage English's
typescript (q.v.), available in the Montserrat Public Library and at the Institute of
Commonwealth Studies library in London, and the printed compilations of Aubrey
Gwynn (q.v.). The author ascribes Irish origin to a number of cultural features in

73

Montserrat, and argues that phenotype, motor habits and accent may all be traced to Ireland, even if specific Irish traits constitute but a small part of the total culture. His arguments are not persuasive because many features he proposes as Irish (for example, goat stew) are widely distributed in Caribbean islands where Irish influence is improbable. Further, the analysis of Montserrat's creole language done by the linguistic scholar J. C. Wells, 'The brogue that isn't' (q.v.), shows that nothing in Montserratian speech or language save a single word can be attributed to Irish influence.

282 **Montserrat 'colony of Ireland': the myth and the reality.**
Howard A. Fergus. *Studies: An Irish Quarterly Review*, Winter 1981, p. 325-40.

Fergus presents a point of view on the Irishness of Montserrat that is very different to that which John C. Messenger expresses in 'The influence of the Irish in Montserrat' (q.v.). He argues convincingly that the Irish role has been sentimentalized and that most of the Irish Catholics, as second-class citizens in an indisputably English colony, were hardly in a position to impose cultural hegemony on black slaves. The evidence offered by Riva Berleant-Schiller in 'Free labor and the economy in seventeenth-century Montserrat' (q.v.) supports Fergus's view.

283 **The influence of the Irish on Montserrat.**
John C. Messenger. *Caribbean Quarterly*, vol. 13, no. 2 (1967), p. 3-26.

A large part of this article is made up of extended quotations from the work of Aubrey Gwynn (q.v.). Most of what is ethnographic and interpretive can be found in Messenger's other 1967 article, 'The Black Irish of Montserrat' (q.v.).

284 **Montserrat: the most distinctively Irish settlement in the New World.**
John C. Messenger. *Ethnicity*, vol. 2, no. 3 (1975), p. 281- 303.

The author writes about the 'two centuries of genetic and cultural exchange between Irish and Africans' that resulted in the putatively Afro-Irish culture and population on the island today. The author bases his interpretation of Irishness in contemporary Montserrat culture on field research, but for his historical review he relies on secondary sources, the undocumented typescript of T. Savage English (q.v.), and the well-documented transcriptions and articles of Aubrey Gwynn (q.v.). No original manuscript sources are cited, even though he describes his work as 'ethnohistorical' (p. 281).

Folklore and literature

285 **Dreams of Alliouagana: an anthology of Montserrat prose and poetry.**
Edited by Howard A. Fergus. Plymouth, Montserrat: University of
the West Indies Centre, 1977. 127p.

Just as the title suggests, this volume includes prose and poetry written by
Montserratians and collected by Dr. Fergus, who teaches at the University of the West
Indies extramural centre in Montserrat.

286 **Folk-lore of the Antilles, French and English.**
Elsie Clews Parsons. New York: American Folk-lore Society, 1933-
36. 3 vols. (Memoirs of the American Folk-lore Society, vol. 26).

In three volumes and two parts, this seminal work is essential for an understanding of
the oral literature of the Antilles. The section devoted to Montserrat is in Part II,
p. 284-307.

287 **Horrors of a hurricane.**
Edited by Howard A. Fergus. Plymouth, Montserrat: University of
the West Indies Centre, 1990. 104p.

Hurricane Hugo devastated several Caribbean islands in September, 1989, but hit none
so hard as Montserrat, where ninety-nine per cent of all residents were left homeless.
This volume is an anthology of poems that were written out of the Montserratian
hurricane experience.

The jombee dance of Montserrat.
See item no. 290.

Religion and cultural identity: the Montserratian case.
See item no. 294.

Caribbean Review.
See item no. 325.

Religion

288 **The death of the jombee dance.**
    Jay. D. Dobbin. Paper presented at the 21st Annual Meeting of the African Studies Association, Baltimore, Maryland, 1978. 18p.

The author argues that underlying the surface of West Indian, Christian, colonial culture in Montserrat is 'a cult which is distinctively African both in its general pattern and particular features' (p. 1). This cult is the jombee dance, the Montserratian form of obeah folk religion found throughout Afro-America. Its disappearance as Montserrat modernizes leaves a cultural gap, since nothing can replace its unique expression of African world view in Montserrat. The author describes the beliefs, rituals, music, preparations and foods that are part of the dance, and describes in detail an actual trance dance that he witnessed. A copy of the paper is on file at the Montserrat National Trust, Montserrat, West Indies.

289 **The jombee dance: friendship and ritual in Montserrat.**
    Jay D. Dobbin. *Caribbean Review*, vol. 10 (1981), p. 28-31.

The Montserratian jombee dance, the local form of obeah religion that is so widely known in Afro-America, served many functions in addition to its stated purpose of propitiating *jombees*, or the dead. During slavery, the practice of obeah was a form of resistance. Now, although the focus of the dance is the healing of an afflicted person, the dancers effectively enact a ritual drama that allows emotional expression and strengthens ties of friendship and kinship.

290 **The jombee dance of Montserrat.**
    Jay D. Dobbin. Columbus, Ohio: Ohio State University Press, 1986. 202p. maps. bibliog.

This book is subtitled 'A study of trance ritual in the West Indies'. It is based on research carried out from 1975 to 1978 into a Montserratian folk religion that is partially derived from African sources and that belongs to the generic class of Afro-American belief systems known collectively as obeah. *Jombees* are ancestral spirits that are active in the material world, making their presence known in sacred objects and in dreams and trances. The jombee dance itself is the central event in the celebration that also includes song, instrumental music, food and drink. The ritual culminates in the dancers' achievement of trance. It is now performed very rarely, but was important in strengthening ties of kinship and friendship, providing an opportunity to work out personal problems and instilling a sense of Montserratian identity. This book succeeds in describing a significant though waning aspect of Montserrat culture, setting it in the larger context of folk religions and showing its multicultural origins.

291 **Review of** *The jombee dance of Montserrat.*
Leslie G. Desmangles. *Anthropos*, vol. 83 (1988), p. 558-90.

This review of Jay Dobbin's book (q.v.) summarizes it intelligently, and points to the following deficiencies: actual historical data that might clarify how and why African and Christian religions combined in Montserrat are lacking; a theoretical framework for the culture creolization process is absent. Nevertheless, the book receives high praise for dedicated and competent research in the under-researched area of contemporary Caribbean religions.

292 **Review of** *The jombee dance of Montserrat.*
Loftur R. Gissurarson. *Sociological Analysis*, vol. 50 (1989), p. 195-97.

Gissurarson concludes that Dobbin's book (q.v.) is a worthwhile and interesting description of a trance dance and a dying folk religion, but objects to the fact that Dobbin's interpretations of the dance cannot be disproved.

293 **Review of** *The jombee dance of Montserrat.*
Stephen D. Glazier. *Journal of American Folklore*, vol. 100 (1987), p. 363-65.

This review summarizes the content of Dobbin's book (q.v.) and praises the author for painstaking research. Glazier takes issue, however, with the absence of details concerning the author's own interactions with informants, and his contention that the jombee dance is dying out. Glazier thinks that a transformation of the dance is more likely, since similar kinds of religious phenomena have flourished elsewhere in the Caribbean despite modernization and westernization.

294 **Religion and cultural identity: the Montserratian case.**
Jay D. Dobbin. *Caribbean Issues*, vol. 4, no. 1 (1980), p. 71-83.

The author argues that important aspects of Montserratian culture are disappearing with modernization, that these are significant to the cultural and national identity of Montserratians, and that these features have been preserved in Montserratian folk religion and ritual. Folk religion has been central to Montserratian identity since long before emancipation, when its forbidden practice expressed rebellion and resistance and permitted creative expression in music, dance and ritual. As the practice of folk religion dwindles, so too does Montserrat's distinctiveness and its people's sense of a distinctive identity.

295 **The Catholic Church in Montserrat, West Indies, 1756-1980.**
Bishop Antoine Demets. Plymouth, Montserrat: Montserrat Printery, 1980. 69p.

This brief history was compiled from parish records surviving from 1756, although the first Irish Catholics arrived in 1632. It includes a chronological list of all the Catholic priests who served in Montserrat from 1756 to 1980, and mentions names of Catholic parishioners. Irish, French, Belgian and North American priests have all served. The Roman Catholic Church, St. Patrick's, and the greatest majority of Roman Catholic communicants are located in the southern parish of Montserrat, St. Patrick's.

296 **Saint Anthony's Church, Montserrat, W.I.**

Fred E. Peters. Bridgetown, Barbados: Advocate Co., 1931. 11p.

A brief history and description of Montserrat's Anglican church, St. Anthony's, located in the town of Plymouth. Although the building has been replaced, St. Anthony's is the first church of which we have record, founded shortly after the first English colonization in the seventeenth century.

297 **The origin of Judy Piece Methodism in the island of Montserrat, B.W.I.**

George E. Lawrence. Plymouth, Montserrat: no imprint, 1944. 29p.

Judy Piece is a rural Montserrat village with a local history of Methodism. This booklet traces the history of Judy Piece Methodism to its nineteenth-century origins. More on this subject can be found in Lawrence's *Thomas O'Garra: a West Indian local preacher*.

298 **Thomas O'Garra: a West Indian local preacher.**

George E. Lawrence. London: Epworth Press, [n.d.]. 59p.

A brief biographical and character sketch of Thomas O'Garra, a Methodist minister of the twentieth century who was associated with Judy Piece Methodism in northern Montserrat.

The first Irish priests in the new world.

See item no. 280.

Education

299 **Education in Montserrat.**
T. E. Ryan. *Corona*, vol. 14, no. 1 (1962), p. 15-18.
This article explains the educational policy that Great Britain established for Montserrat in 1945, when a free public education system replaced a system run by the churches.

300 **The implications of size for educational development in small countries: Montserrat, a Caribbean case study.**
M. Bray, Howard M. Fergus. *Compare*, vol. 16, no. 1 (1986), p. 91-102.
Even though Montserrat is a colony of Great Britain and small in size, it has long had a high degree of autonomy. It is therefore comparable to many of the microstates that have recently gained independent status. The authors compare the social and political influences that shape education in Montserrat with the influences in a selection of small but viable independent states, and discuss the problems and the advantages of small size.

301 **Restructuring education in Montserrat and St. Kitts.**
Howard A. Fergus. *Caribbean Journal of Education*, vol. 14, no. 1-2 (1987), p. 163-77.
This paper is a response to documents issued by the governments of Montserrat and St. Kitts concerning the relationship of education to the need for economic development. Fergus points out that the government assessment of economic trends was derived solely from a very short-term study of ongoing economic activities; therefore the list that the documents present of educational ideals usually associated with those activities might not be wholly appropriate for development and innovation. Fergus, an historian who teaches at the University of the West Indies extramural extension in Montserrat, closes with suggestions for an effective educational strategy for the two islands.

Statistics

302 **An abstract of the statistics of the Leeward Islands, Windward Islands, and Barbados.**
Carleen O'Loughlin. Mona, Jamaica: Institute of Social and Economic Research (ISER), University of the West Indies, 1966. 73p.
This statistical abstract is useful for historical economic statistics and for comparing Montserrat with other islands of the Lesser Antilles.

303 **Government of Montserrat statistical digest. Vol. 1- . 1972- .**
Plymouth, Montserrat: Statistics Office, 1973- . annual.
This is the official source for statistics of all kinds relating to Montserrat. It includes tabular information on such topics as income, housing, population composition, vital statistics, migration, employment, construction, trade, agriculture, tourism, education, banking, communications, finance, labour unions, public health, and the income and expenses of the government.

304 **National accounts statistics, 1975-1982.**
Plymouth, Montserrat: Statistics Office, 1983. 38p.
This compilation consists of thirty-four tables on Montserrat's economy and economic growth. It provides information on gross domestic production, national income, employment and unemployment, and public and private economic sectors. Each table provides comparison figures from 1975 to 1982 inclusive.

305 **Overseas trade report. Vol. 1- . 1970- .**
Plymouth, Montserrat: Statistics Office, 1971- . annual.
This report collates the most important statistics on imports and exports for the year, with comparison figures for previous years. A brief commentary summarizes the tables, which are based on customs documents.

306   **Report on prices, trade and tourism. Vol. 1- . 1977- .**
Plymouth, Montserrat: Statistics Office, 1978- . annual.
The information in this government publication may also be found in the annual
Statistical Digest (q.v.) and the annual *Tourism Report* (q.v.).

307   **Tourism report. Vol. 1- . 1977- .**
Plymouth, Montserrat: Statistics Office, 1978- . annual.
This report is a tabular statistical summary with brief commentary, based on
Immigration Office records. It provides information on the number of tourists who
entered each year, where they came from, where and how long they stayed, how they
travelled, and estimates of how much money they spent on the island. The information
is not exactly the same every year. In 1982, for example, the report began to include a
count of hotel beds available on the island.

Newspapers and Periodicals

Newspapers

308 **Caribbean Business.**
San Juan, Puerto Rico: Casiano Communications, 1973- . weekly.
A source of general business and economic news for the Caribbean region, this newspaper also includes advertisements, information on travel, occasional special features and an index. Its circulation is about 42,500.

309 **Caribbean Contact.**
Bridgetown, Barbados: Caribbean Contact Ltd., 1973- . monthly.
This monthly regional newspaper is published in and for the Caribbean, and thus provides a good source for Caribbean views on Caribbean events. Its circulation is about 23,000 and it includes advertising and book reviews as well as regional news.

310 **Caribbean Times.**
London: Hansib Publications, 1981- . weekly.
This newspaper caters for the interests of Caribbean peoples living in the United Kingdom. A special feature is its regular film reviews. The circulation is about 25,000.

311 **The Montserrat Reporter.**
Plymouth, Montserrat: Montserrat Reporter. weekly on Fridays.
This is one of the two weekly newspapers published in Montserrat that reports local news and politics. Its circulation is about 2,000.

312   **The Montserrat Times.**
      Plymouth, Montserrat: Montserrat Times. weekly on Fridays.
This is one of the two weekly newspapers published in Montserrat that covers local
news and politics. It has a circulation of about 1,000.

Periodicals

313   **Bulletin of Eastern Caribbean Affairs.**
      Cave Hill, Barbados: Institute of Social and Economic Research
      (Eastern Caribbean), 1974- . bimonthly.
This important journal publishes 'informed and analytical commentaries on significant
political, social and economic developments in the Caribbean, with special emphasis on
Eastern Caribbean states'. It includes reports on conferences and research projects,
news items from each eastern Caribbean state, texts of significant speeches, news of
the Organization of Eastern Caribbean States and book reviews.

314   **Cajanus.**
      Mona, Jamaica: Food and Nutrition Institute of the University of the
      West Indies, 1967- . quarterly.
The publication of this journal is funded by the Pan-American Health Organization
and the World Health Organization. It publishes research articles on nutrition and
diet, with emphasis on the population of the Caribbean. Circulation is about 2,000.

315   **Caribbean Affairs.**
      Port of Spain, Trinidad and Tobago: Trinidad Express, 1972- . quarterly.
This literary and political quarterly features news, information, and discussion of issues
of interest to the entire Caribbean Basin, from the coast of Brazil to the Bahamas. It is
written by Caribbean people for the Caribbean region, and is thus a good source for
Caribbean views on Caribbean literary and political life. It has a circulation of about
850.

316   **Caribbean Conservation News.**
      St. Michael, Barbados: Caribbean Conservation Association, 1975- .
      quarterly.
Formerly entitled the *Caribbean Conservation Association Newsletter*, this publication
appears four times a year, circulates to about 800 subscribers, and incudes articles and
book reviews on the topic of the conservation of Caribbean environments and
resources.

317   **Caribbean Dateline.**
      Washington DC: Caribbean Dateline Publications, 1980- . monthly.
This is a loose-leaf business and investment news and advisory service that circulates to
about 1,200. It frequently includes news of business and finance in Montserrat.

318 **Caribbean Directory.**
Castries, St. Lucia: Caribbean Publishing Co., 1979- . annual.
Provides an annually updated listing of trade and manufacturing firms in the
Caribbean. It includes advertising and has a circulation of about 20,000.

319 **Caribbean Economic Almanac.**
Port of Spain, Trinidad and Tobago: Economic and Business Research
Information and Advisory Service, 1962- . irregular.
This is an irregularly published source of economic and statistical data about the
Caribbean region that is useful for those who carry on international commerce. It
includes reviews of new books and has a circulation of about 1,000.

320 **Caribbean Geography.**
Kingston, Jamaica: Longman Jamaica, 1983- . annual.
This periodical, edited by David Barker and Michael Morrissey of the University of the
West Indies, publishes geographical research articles on the Caribbean region. It has a
circulation of about 300.

321 **Caribbean Handbook.**
St. John's, Antigua: F. T. Caribbean, 1983- . annual.
This yearly review of business and economics in the Caribbean region functions as a
handbook for carrying on business and as a directory to business in the Caribbean. It
also includes advertising and book reviews, and has a circulation of about 9,000.

322 **Caribbean Insight.**
London: West India Committee, 1977- . monthly.
This monthly is a continuation of the former *Caribbean Chronicle*, which itself
continued the *West Indies Chronicle*. It is an excellent source for information about
political and economic developments in the region, and for Caribbean international
economic relations. Montserrat news appears regularly. The circulation is about 3,000.

323 **Caribbean Monthly Bulletin.**
Río Piedras, Puerto Rico: Institute of Caribbean Studies of the
University of Puerto Rico, 1963- . monthly.
Published in English, Spanish and French, this monthly has individual sections on
separate Caribbean nations, and a 'News in Brief' section for those territories not
covered in detail in that particular issue, and for pan-Caribbean organizations, such as
Caricom, Caribbean Development Bank and Organization of Eastern Caribbean
States. The periodical offers mainly economic and political news to about 1,500
subscribers. It is an excellent source for news about the internal affairs and
international relationships of Caribbean countries, and almost always has at least a
short section on Montserrat. Its drawback is that it sometimes falls behind its
publication schedule.

324 **Caribbean Quarterly.**
Kingston, Jamaica: University of the West Indies, Department of
Extra-Mural Studies, 1949- . quarterly.
This is a general review that includes articles on Caribbean history, literature,
economics, politics and agriculture. It is indexed, is available on microfilm, and
includes book reviews and advertising. The circulation is about 1,500.

325 **Caribbean Review.**
Miami, Florida: Caribbean Review, 1969- . quarterly.
This quarterly is devoted to the Caribbean and Latin America, and to emigrant groups
from these countries living elsewhere. It includes essays on a wide range of cultural,
social, political and economic topics, research articles, fiction, art and literary criticism,
news about the arts and book reviews. The circulation is about 5,000.

326 **Caribbean Studies.**
Río Piedras, Puerto Rico: Institute of Caribbean Studies, 1961- .
quarterly.
A scholarly journal devoted to research articles on social and economic topics related
to the Caribbean region. Its circulation is about 1,500.

327 **Caribbean Tourism Statistical Report.**
Christ Church, Barbados: Caribbean Tourism Research and
Development Centre, 1978- . annual.
Formerly called *Caribbean Tourism Statistics*, this periodical is useful as an annually
updated collection of statistics related to the tourism industry. Its circulation is about
1,000.

328 **Caribbean Trend Watch.**
Port Washington, New York: Hank Boerner, 1986- . monthly.
Formerly called *Carib-Basin Trade Update*, this is a monthly service for business
people in the United States who carry on trade in the Caribbean region.

329 **Caribbean Update.**
Maplewood, New Jersey: Kal Wagenheim, 1985- . monthly.
Current circulation is controlled by the publisher, but back issues are available from
the publisher at 52 Maple Avenue, Maplewood, New Jersey, USA, 07040. This
monthly covers business and economic news in the Caribbean and Central America,
and is useful for international commerce. It frequently covers developments in
Montserrat.

330 **Caricom Perspective.**
Georgetown, Guyana: Caribbean Community Secretariat, 1980- .
bimonthly.
This valuable publication of the Caribbean Community covers regional economic
conditions. Subscriptions are available free from the Caricom Secretariat, PO Box
10827, Georgetown, Guyana. Back issues are also available. Circulation is about 6,000.

331 **Social and Economic Studies.**
Mona, Jamaica: Institute for Social and Economic Research, University of the West Indies, 1953- . quarterly.

This is an important scholarly journal devoted to international historical and social scientific research on Caribbean topics. It is available on microfilm, includes book reviews and circulates to 2,000 subscribers.

Reference Sources

332 Biographical dictionary of Latin American and Caribbean political leaders.
Edited by Robert Alexander. Westport, Connecticut: Greenwood Press, 1987. 505p. bibliog.
The main body of this volume is an alphabetic listing of brief biographies by surname. An appendix indexes all biographies by country or territory. Montserrat's important figures include Percival Austin Bramble, William Henry Bramble and John Alfred Osborne, chief minister since 1978.

333 Caribbean Personalities.
Edited by Anthony Lancelot Levy, Hedley Powell Jacobs. Kingston, Jamaica: Caribbean Personalities, 1970- . biennial.
This is a guide to public personalities in the Caribbean. It is published once every two years, is arranged alphabetically by country, and includes biographical data in *Who's Who* style.

334 The CARICOM bibliography.
Caribbean Community Secretariat. Information and Documentation Section. Georgetown, Guyana: CARICOM Secretariat, 1977- . annual.
This ongoing bibliography is published annually, usually in two numbers. It includes references to works related to member states, including Montserrat.

335 The Complete Caribbeana, 1900-1975: a bibliographic guide to the scholarly literature.
Lambros Comitas. Millwood, New York: KTO Press, 1977. 4 vols.
A comprehensive bibliography of works relating to the Lesser Antilles, Jamaica, the Guyanas and Surinam, and the Caribbean littoral of Central America, but excluding Haiti, Puerto Rico, Cuba and the Dominican Republic. There are more than 17,000

Reference Sources

entries for works in English, French, Dutch, German, Spanish, Russian, Swedish, Danish and Papiamento. These are arranged topically, with a geographical and author cross-index. The bibliography also lists periodicals published about and in the Caribbean, and archives and libraries containing Caribbean collections. It contains additional references to Montserrat that have not been selected for the present volume.

336 Directory of Caribbeanists.

Sylvia Potter. Rio Piedras, Puerto Rico: Interamerican University of Puerto Rico: Caribbean Studies Association, 1989. 73p.

A list of researchers and scholars working on Caribbean topics. The list includes their research loci, and locates those working or having worked in Montserrat.

337 A guide for the study of British Caribbean history, 1763- 1834.

Lowell Joseph Ragatz. Washington, DC: Unites States Government Printing Office, 1932. 725p.

This is an essential guide for anyone wishing to do research in the history of the British Caribbean, including Montserrat. It includes an extensive classified, annotated list of periodical articles, books and manuscript sources indexed by author, title and subject.

338 Historical dictionary of the British Caribbean.

William Lux. Metuchen, New Jersey, 1975. 266p. bibliog.

This volume covers the English-speaking areas of the Caribbean Basin and littoral. Each area is given a separate section, and regional political units are treated collectively. Thus Montserrat is treated in the Leeward Islands section. The volume is arranged alphabetically by topic and covers agriculture, law, geographical locations, newspapers, persons, business firms, education, government and religion, all dealt with historically.

339 Islands of the Commonwealth Caribbean: a regional study.

Edited by Sandra W. Meditz, Dennis M. Hanratty. Washington, DC: Library of Congress, 1989. 771p.

Research on this handbook was completed in 1987. It covers history, population, statistics, health, education, economy, government, politics, foreign relations and security. The coverage of recent political and economic events is good, but the information on cultural, social, historical and governmental topics is weak, and was gleaned from outdated and unreliable sources, even where better information was readily available. Consequently the volume is full of errors. The bibliographies for each island show insufficient knowledge of the literature on the part of the editors, and are inadequate for a volume that proposes itself as a current authoritative source.

340 Political parties of the Americas.

Edited by Robert Alexander. Westport, Connecticut: Greenwood Press, 1983. 2 vols.

This reference source summarizes the history and nature of political parties in all of the states of the Americas, arranged by country. The entry for Montserrat is in the second volume, and is the best single source for gaining an understanding of the history of Montserratian party politics.

341   **South America, Central America, and the Caribbean.**
      London: Europa Publications, 1991. 3rd ed. 702p. bibliog.
This is the third edition of the standard handbook on the political and economic life of
Latin America and the Caribbean. The entry on Montserrat includes a summary of
statistical information, a description of government, and reviews of banking, trade,
industry and transport.

Indexes

There follow three separate indexes: authors (personal and corporate); titles; and subjects. Title entries are italicized and refer to either the main titles, or to other works cited in the annotations. The numbers refer to bibliographic entry rather than page numbers. Individual index entries are arranged in alphabetical sequence.

Index of Authors

Index of Titles

A

Abstract of the statistics of the Leeward Islands, Windward Islands, and Barbados 302
Acts of assembly, passed in the island of Montserrat; from 1668 to 1740, inclusive 209
African exchange: toward a biological history of black people 128
Agricultural soils of Montserrat 232
Alliouagana in focus 1
Ancient native America 112

B

Behold the West Indies 32
Beiträge zur regionalen Geologie der Erde. Vol. 4: Geologie der Antillen 41
Biographical dictionary of Latin American and Caribbean political leaders 332
Birds of Montserrat 95
Birds of the West Indies 96
Birnbaum's Caribbean 37
Blathwayt atlas 23
British empire in America 137
Bulletin of eastern Caribbean affairs 313
Butterflies and other insects of the eastern Caribbean 105

C

Cajanus 314
Calendar of state papers, colonial series, America and the West Indies, 1574-1737 129
Carib-Basin Trade Update 328
Caribbean Affairs 315
Caribbean Business 308
Caribbean Chronicle 322
Caribbean Conservation News 316
Caribbean Contact 309
Caribbean Contours 276
Caribbean Dateline 317
Caribbean Directory 318
Caribbean Economic Almanac 319
Caribbean Geography 320
Caribbean Handbook 321
Caribbean Insight 322
Caribbean Islands 11
Caribbean Monthly Bulletin 323
Caribbean Personalities 333
Caribbean Quarterly 324
Caribbean Review 325
Caribbean Studies 326
Caribbean Times 310
Caribbean Tourism Statistical Report 327
Caribbean Transformations 168
Caribbean Trend Watch 328
Caribbean Update 329
Caribbeana 130, 143
Caricom bibliography 334
Caricom perspective 330
Catalog of the active volcanoes of the world. Part XX, West Indies 66
Catholic church in Montserrat, West Indies, 1756-1980 295
Chronologies in new world archaeology 110
Commercial geography of Montserrat 12
Commissioners' report on justice 210

Complete Caribbeana, 1900-1975 335
Contributions to the regional geology of the earth. Vol. 4: geology of the Antilles 41
Corporations and society 175
Cruising guide to the Lesser Antilles 38

D

Data atlas for Montserrat 3
Demographic survey of the British colonial empire: vol. III, West Indian and American territories 164
Development of the British West Indies, 1700-1763 149
Development of the Leeward Islands under the Restoration, 1660-1688 139
Diary of John Baker 150
Directory of Caribbeanists 336
Dreams of Alliouagana: an anthology of Montserrat prose and poetry 285

E

Environmental guidelines for development in the Lesser Antilles 79

F

Field guide to the butterflies of the West Indies 108
Fielding's Caribbean 39

95

Index of Subjects

A

Absentee landlords 148
Africa 128, 168, 288, 296
Agave species 82
Agency for International
    Development 228
Agriculture 14, 237-273
    commodities 161, 235,
        246-254
    cotton 246-248, 250-251,
        253, 265-266
    crop loss 271
    departments of 273
    development 216, 218,
        223, 240, 242-244, 265-
        273
    farmers 240, 243
    food crops 245, 271-272
    forage crops 267
    limes 161, 235, 249, 251,
        254, 265-266
    livestock 256, 262, 265-
        267, 270
    maize 237
    peppers 257, 259
    pests and diseases 254-
        264
    shifting cultivation 238
    small plot cultivation 14,
        239-245, 271-272
    statistics 303
    tomatoes 255, 261
    women in 178
Airport 217
Amelioration *see* Slavery
Amerindians *see*
    Archaeology
Amphibians 104
Anaemia 192
Anglican Church 72, 296
Anguilla 107, 116
Animals 7, 93-109
    see also Agriculture,
        livestock
Anthropology 6, 9, 167-
    190, 274-294
    see also Archaeology

Antigua 107, 142, 159, 201,
    226, 237, 243, 246-247,
    263, 270
Archaeology 119-127
    Montserrat after 1492
        120-127
    Montserrat before 1492
        115-119
    regional 110-114, 116
Architecture 72, 296
Art 325

B

Baker, John 150
Banking fraud 222, 224-
    225, 231
Barbados 226, 229, 246-247
Barbuda 107, 116-118, 159,
    226, 245
Bats 93
Belize 226
Bibliographies 334-335,
    337
    agriculture 245, 269
    volcanic eruptions 264
Biography 208, 298, 332-
    333
Birds 94-98
Blacks 128
Bramble, Percival Austin
    332
Bramble, William Henry
    204, 208, 332
British Virgin Islands 50
British West Indies 36,
    133, 144, 146, 148-149,
    154, 158, 160, 164,
    234, 273, 338-339
    see also Commonwealth
        Caribbean; Leeward
        Islands Colony;
        Names of individual
        islands or colonies,
        e.g. British Virgin
        Islands
Budget 217, 303-304

Business directories 318
Business periodicals 308,
    317, 319, 321, 328-329
Butterflies 105-106, 108

C

Canada 179
Caribbean Basin 45-46, 53
Caribbean Community
    (CARICOM) 202,
    226, 330, 334
Caribbean culture 167-169,
    172, 325
Caribbean region
    see British West Indies;
        Commonwealth
        Caribbean; English
        America; Greater
        Antilles; Leeward
        Islands Colony; Lesser
        Antilles; West Indies;
        Names of individual
        islands or territories,
        e.g. Barbuda.
Caribbean society 167-169,
    171-172, 175
CARICOM *See* Caribbean
    Community
Catholic Church 72, 295
Census 130, 143
Children's health 195, 201
Churches 72, 295-298
Class and stratification 9,
    146, 155, 168, 170,
    172-176, 181
Colonial status 4, 202-203,
    206
Colonialism 158, 168, 172,
    203, 206
Commonwealth Caribbean
    339
    See also British West
        Indies
Communications 303
Conservation 79-81, 316
Constitution 205

99

Ryan, Mary 150

S

Saba 44, 47
Sailing 39
St. Christopher 106, 140,
142
see also St. Kitts
St. Eustatius 44
St. Kitts 44, 107, 159, 226,
229, 237, 240, 263, 301
see also St.
Christopher
St. Lucia 226, 229, 240
St. Martin 116
St. Vincent 226, 244
Schistosomiasis 196-197,
199
Scorpions 109
Sharecropping 265
Shells 101, 103
Slave trade 139, 154
Slavery 35, 144, 146-147,
149, 155, 157, 167-168,
210-211
amelioration 152, 210
Slaves 128, 144, 146, 150
burial grounds 120, 122,
124
education 152
emancipation 36, 159,
162
health and disease 122,
154
population 143, 154
religion 152, 299
see also Freed slaves
Social change 6, 183
Social organization 9, 169-
172

see also Family;
Household
organization; Kinship
Social science periodicals
326, 331
Social structure *see* Class
and stratification
Society 1, 6, 8-9, 170, 186-
188
see also Class and
stratification; Social
organization
Soil 232-236
erosion 238
fertility 237
South America 112, 114,
341
Spirit possession 288-294
Standard of living 217
Stapleton, William 136,
143, 145, 156
Statistics 302-307, 319, 327
vital 154, 164, 303
Soufrière Hills 54, 56, 78
Sugar 123, 146
plantations 121, 125,
153, 156-157
production and export
151, 265, 266

T

Tierra del Fuego 112
Tobago 87, 226
Topography 51
Tourism 3,7, 25-31, 216,
218, 223
statistics 174, 272, 303,
306-307, 327
tourist divorce 215
Trant's Estate 115, 239

Travel guides 37-40
Travellers' accounts 32-36,
62
Trees 89
Trinidad 87, 201, 226
Tuberculosis 200

V

Veterinary medicine 256,
262
Vital statistics *see*
Statistics, vital
Volcanic eruptions 64, 76
Volcanoes and volcanology
43, 48, 51, 54-63, 66,
71, 75, 77-78

W

West Indies 20, 64, 76, 82,
96, 108, 111, 135, 140,
157, 253, 257, 273
see also British West
Indies; Greater
Antilles; Leeward
Islands Colony; Lesser
Antilles; names of
individual islands and
colonies, e.g.
Barbuda.
Women 176-177, 180
employment of 179, 181
in agriculture 178
in politics 205

Y

Yucatán 114

102

Map of Montserrat

This map shows the more important towns and other features.

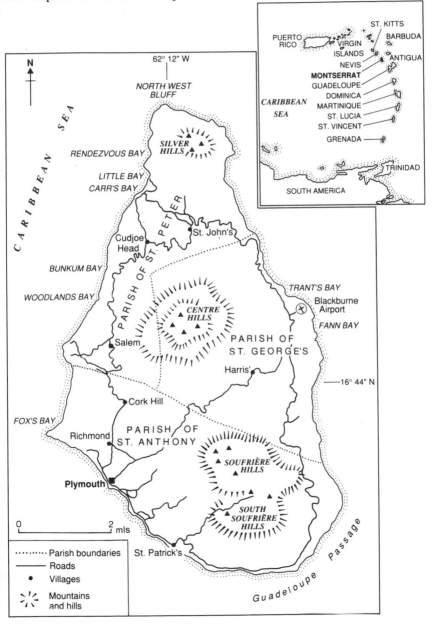

N

62° 12" W

NORTH WEST
BLUFF

ST. KITTS
PUERTO
RICO
VIRGIN
ISLANDS
BARBUDA
ANTIGUA
NEVIS
MONTSERRAT
GUADELOUPE
CARIBBEAN
SEA
DOMINICA
MARTINIQUE
ST. LUCIA
ST. VINCENT
GRENADA
TRINIDAD
SOUTH AMERICA

CARIBBEAN SEA

SILVER
HILLS

RENDEZVOUS BAY

LITTLE BAY
CARR'S BAY

PARISH OF ST. PETER

Cudjoe
Head
St. John's

BUNKUM BAY

WOODLANDS BAY

TRANT'S BAY
Blackburne
Airport
FANN BAY

CENTRE
HILLS

Salem

PARISH OF
ST. GEORGE'S

Harris'

—16° 44" N

Cork Hill

FOX'S BAY

Richmond

PARISH OF
ST. ANTHONY

SOUFRIÈRE
HILLS

Plymouth

SOUTH
SOUFRIÈRE
HILLS

0   2 mls

.... Parish boundaries
———— Roads
•   Villages
Mountains
and hills

St. Patrick's

Guadeloupe Passage